THE
FUNNY
THING
ABOUT
STRESS

THE FUNNY THING ABOUT STRESS

A SERIOUSLY HUMOROUS
GUIDE TO A HAPPIER LIFE

KAY FRANCES, MBA

Morton-Wells Press

Morton-Wells|Press

All other inquiries can be made to: www.MortonWells.com

The following trademarks appear throughout this book: AP, Black & Decker, Budgetel, Cadillac, Cheetos, Clove gum, Cocoa Puffs, Coke Zero, Diet Coke, *Extreme Makeover*, H&R Block, *Hamlet*, Hilton Hotel, HoHo's, IBM, *Jeopardy*, Lasix, Peanut M&M's, McDonald's, Microsoft, Midol, Motel 6, Oh Mama!, *One Flew Over the Cuckoo's Nest*, Pampered Chef, *Psycho*, *Rebecca of Sunnybrook Farm*, Scrabble, S&H Green Stamps, S.O.S. pad, SAG Harbor, SPAM, *The Da Vinci Code*, Teflon, *The Wizard of Oz*, *Titanic*, Tupperware, U-Scan, Volkswagen Beetle, Walmart, *Whistle While You Work*, and YMCA.

Although the author and publisher have exhaustively researched all sources to ensure the accuracy and completeness of the information contained in this book, we assume no responsibility for errors, inaccuracies, omissions or any other inconsistency herein. Any slights against people or organizations are unintentional. Readers should consult a physician or mental healthcare professional for specific information about their individual stress management plan.

To order this book individually or in bulk visit: **www.MortonWells.com**

Printed by Malloy Incorporated in the United States of America
Third Printing, June 2014

Library of Congress Control Number: 2010909118

ISBN-13: 978-0-9845806-0-6
ISBN-10: 0-9845806-0-3

Cover and interior design by James Monroe Design LLC
Cover photograph by Ken Gosney Photography

*With loving memory of Mom and Dad,
this book is dedicated to
Carol, Glenn, Cindy,
Amanda, Kate, and Savannah.*

DISCLAIMER FROM
THE AUTHOR

*T*he information contained in this book is for entertainment purposes and is intended to evoke laughter, curiosity, and questions from the reader. It is not meant to be a substitute for advice from your doctor, psychologist, therapist, psychiatrist, minister, butcher, baker, or candlestick maker. I'm just saying.

When I talk about ambling through red lights, eating SPAM on crackers, leaping off tall buildings, and robbing banks, IT'S A JOKE! I am not encouraging anyone to do these things. Seriously. I'd really rather you didn't. I've got enough to stress over. But, if you think that reading my little tome might tempt you to commit these heinous acts, please step awaaaay from the book!

I mean really.

*"A clown is like an aspirin,
except that it works twice as fast."*

—Groucho Marx

CONTENTS

ACKNOWLEDGMENTS

Wow! Where do I begin? If I listed all of the people who have impacted my life and made this book possible, this section would be longer than the book itself! And without all of my life experiences to date—both good and not-so-good—I would have nothing to write about. So, I guess I'm feeling a lot of gratitude for life in general!

More specifically, I would like to offer a huge THANK YOU to the people who were most instrumental in helping me get this book from my heart and head to paper. With their wisdom, generosity, humor, insight, encouragement, tough love, support, and "fresh eyes," I was able to see this book through to completion.

First, I want to express my appreciation to the fine professionals who helped bring this book to life: James Monroe, Ken Gosney, Amy Quale, and the wonderful folks at Malloy Incorporated. Thank you! I'm in awe of the work that you do.

Hugs and "Hollywood air kisses" to my siblings, Carol Thomas, Glenn Brewer, and Cindy Brewer for their ongoing love and their support of my wild schemes over the years. Thank you to Mellody Russo (Mel-DEEE!) for her steadfast (almost supernatural) support of me and this project. If this book is my "baby," it's Mel-D's godchild.

A gigantic "thank you" to Colleen "Tap, Tap" Delegan, author and friend extraordinaire. She cut my learning curve by offering her professional opinion each time I found myself drowning in a pool of confusion. Her kindness, friendship and generous spirit do not go unappreciated! I also want to express my gratitude for the help I got from award-winning authors and squash aficionados (squash the game, not the vegetable) John Baskin and Michael Graham. They patiently allowed me to accost them at the YMCA with my endless parade of questions.

Thanks and a big hug to Barbara "Mama B" Kneisel for being my friend and biggest cheerleader on this project. Kudos to R.D. Lawrence (a fine author in his own right) for his off-beat sense of humor and valuable suggestions.

Many, many thanks to Tammy "Eagle Eye" McKay for her help and encouragement. I'm also extremely grateful for the detailed analysis, honesty, humor, friendship and education I received from author and financial guru Ken Robinson.

I'm so fortunate to have a lot of great friends who weighed in with opinions on design choices and content. I very much appreciate them taking the time to give me their input, support and advice. Many thanks to: Tim Angel, Brenda Asterino, Susie Chaney, Laura Curliss, Ken Driscoll, Patti Driscoll, Patrick

Gentile, Greg "Flash" Gordon, Sharon Griffith, Frank Hale, Judy Hatfield, Tom Ibaugh, Jo Ann Knable, Mark Knable, Deb Kneisel, Christine Krisa, Debbie Leonard, Jim Leonard, Dawn Lyon, Dave McCord, Mary McIntosh, Stephanie McIntosh, Lois Minton, Janine Moon, Lisa Newburger, Dan Pinney, Donna Pinney, Brad Reynolds, Rachel Sexton, Stan Tackett, Jean Tipton, Linda Wallingford, Jen Williams, and Robin Weaver.

Thanks to my cat, Seisan for being my ever-faithful companion. She was great company during the writing process, instinctively knowing when to stay and cuddle and when to go away.

To all of the above: you're priceless! I'm a better (and less stressed!) person for having known you all.

My most humble thanks go to the people in my audiences over the years. You inspired me to keep going with your laughter and support, even during the lean years when the going wasn't easy. I'm forever grateful and hope to continue to serve many more people in the future.

REFLECTIONS OF A
RECOVERING STRESSAHOLIC

I'm a corporate dropout. Lord knows I gave the business world a good try, but I just couldn't make it "fit." For one thing, all three companies that I worked for ended up in bankruptcy which kept me in a perpetual state of insecurity. I also grew weary of being moved around the country like a chess piece (including *two* stints in Oklahoma). A lovely state, in fact, the wind does indeed come sweepin' down the plain, just like the song says. But it wasn't "home."

The third time I found myself unemployed, I did the next "logical" thing and became a professional stand-up comedian. (I do hold open the possibility that my checkered life path makes sense only to me.) I had been doing stand-up comedy as a hobby for a couple of years and people were actually offering work to me. It was the early 1980s and the comedy scene was booming. I decided, "I'm going to do this! I'm going to trash my MBA and become a touring stand-up comedian!" Boy were my parents proud. I didn't even know how to tell them. I thought, "I won't come right out and tell them what I do. I'll just describe it to them."

Me: I work late at night and show people a good time.

Folks: Oh my lord. Our daughter's a hooker!

Me: No, no! They laugh when I perform.

Folks: She's a hooker and she's not even good at it!

See, most people who get a master's degree in business administration go to work for IBM or Microsoft, not the Yuk Factory or the Grin Bin. Seriously.

There was nothing about my time in the corporate world that cigarettes, drugs, alcohol, and workaholism couldn't cure. Except boredom and loneliness, particularly during my time in Oklahoma. In my mid-twenties, I was ill-prepared for the stresses of three solitary cross-country moves coupled with being employed by three unstable companies. Add that to my lack of healthy coping skills and it was a perfect storm of stress.

Hitting the road as a stand-up comedian did little to relieve that stress. As a matter of fact, it compounded it. For one thing, when you are self-employed you are constantly scrounging for work. There was no job security whatsoever.

Then there was the travel. It was relentless. I could never figure out how to get the audiences to come to my house, so I had to go to them.

Also, the money wasn't very good. The first year that I went from the corporate world to stand-up comedy, my income fell by 75%. I was audited by the IRS that year. I think the auditor just wanted to ask me face-to-face, "Why? Why would you *do* this?"

Since the money wasn't very good, I had to work a *lot*. As much as humanly possible. I remember a six-week run of "one-nighters" that started in Pennsylvania and ended in Florida. I couldn't keep straight what town I was in from night to night. I'd be onstage and say, "It's nice to be here in, um, where *am* I anyway?" Not the best way to endear yourself to the locals.

Living on the road didn't lend itself to healthy habits, either. Mostly, I ate in restaurants (if you want to call fast food joints "restaurants"; personally, I think that's stretching the concept). The alcohol flowed and drugs were plentiful. Occasionally, a comedy club owner would ask me, "Do you want to be paid in 'green' or 'white'?" meaning marijuana or cocaine. Mostly, I needed the kind of "green" you could use to fill the gas tank. Mostly.

I was one of the "joke gypsies," which is sort of like migrant workers with microphones. Unlike the famous comedians seen on sitcoms and cable television, we were poorly paid and unheralded as we scoured the country for grins and guffaws.

The hotels in which we stayed were usually horrendous; everything but the bloodstains and chalk outlines on the floor. (Okay, sometimes there *were* bloodstains and chalk outlines.) The well-known comedians would get a penthouse suite across town. But for the rest of us, the comedy club owner would cut a deal with the owner of the local Bates Motel for a cheap rate. I never heard that negotiation between the comedy club owner and hotel proprietor, but I imagine it went something like this:

Yeah, I will be having comedians coming to town on a weekly basis I have to put up, but I want to spend as little as possible. So, I want you to put them in that room you'd never give a full-paying customer. You know the room with the bad plumbing, clogged drain, and no hot water, next to the jackhammer testing factory. The one you don't really want to spend much time cleaning or replacing stuff that's broken. The one with the mattress that's so soft you could suffocate just lying down. The one that has been pried open so many times by jealous lovers and drug busts gone bad that the lock no longer works. *That* one.

So, getting a good night's sleep wasn't an option either.

Yet, with all of its trials, there was a lot about living on the road as a comedian that kept me going. In fact, I would say that I felt driven to do it. I formed a "brotherhood" with my fellow comedians and met some of the funniest and most interesting people I'd ever known. I remain friends with many of them to this day.

There was an allure of the stage and a high I got from making people laugh that is hard to describe and even harder to replicate. However, many of my experiences sound downright loony in retrospect. But at the time I overlooked all of the downsides. In fact, if not for having to make enough money to survive, I would've done it for free.

At one point, I decided to move my comedy career along by relocating to New York City. No stress there! Beyond the anxiety of trying to make it in the Big Apple, I had the stress of newness at every turn. I felt like *Rebecca of Sunnybrook Farm* as I tried to navigate the city using modes of transportation that were totally out of my range of experience: busses, trains, and subways. I didn't even know you could make the bus *stop.* I'd end up blocks and blocks beyond where I needed to get off thinking, "I should've just walked."

MUSING

Ah, show biz. Reminds me of that old joke about the guy whose job was to shovel elephant poop for the circus. He complained about it constantly. Finally, one of his fellow shovelers said, **"If you hate it so much, why don't you quit?"** **"What?! And give up show business?!"**

There are stresses inherent with every move, even if it's just across town. Indeed, "change in location" is widely considered one of the "big three" most stressful events in our lives, right up there with "change in job" and "change in marital status." But when you move to a place that feels like a foreign country, your stress level increases exponentially. I knew how to make other people laugh, but I was so intent on building a career and trying to adapt to all of the unfamiliarity that I forgot my own lessons. Like the shoemaker who has no shoes and walks around barefoot, I was a comedian who had forgotten how to laugh. I was so smothered by stress that my emotional, mental, spiritual, and physical health steadily declined.

There came a point when learning to manage my stress was not just a helpful tool for betterment; it was vital for my very survival. It was a long and winding road back to sanity. Sometimes you have to crouch low to leap high. It was a gradual process, but I finally got healthy. And I remembered how to laugh.

So, to summarize: I went from being a drug-using, alcohol-abusing, nicotine-addicted stressaholic to a healthy, clean, sober, semi-sane stress management humorist. I now travel the country sharing the knowledge I've acquired over the years. I'm still a purveyor of grins and guffaws, but I have a bit more to contribute toward helping others manage their stress and take care of their health. I love my work. And the hotels are much nicer now. Nary a bloodstain.

My goal for this book is to relate what I've learned, both from personal experience and from years of studying stress, humor, and wellness. Some chapters are chock-full of comedy; others are a bit more informative. (The chapters that start with "The Funny Thing About" are particularly high-humor zones.) However, I'm never far from my stand-up comedy roots so you won't have to go far without a smile or chuckle. Even when I offer serious stress strategies, humor is the vehicle for the message.

So, relax and enjoy the ride both while reading this book and in your daily life. We might as well be happy, feel good, and get the most out of our lives while we're here. After all, as the old saying goes, "This is just life and none of us gets out of here alive."

Seriously.

PART I

The Funny Thing About Humor:
The "Small" Stuff

···

CHAPTER ONE

Find the Funny in Daily Life

A merry heart doeth good like a medicine:
but a broken spirit drieth the bones.

—Proverbs 17:22

The years I spent as a touring stand-up comedian taught me a lot:

1. A person can actually live out of their car (it was a *glamorous* life).

2. I learned how to exist on Peanut M&M's and gas station hot dogs. (You know how you see those raggedy-looking wieners going around and around for hours? You might wonder, "Who *eats* those things?" Why, I did. Often.)

3. People need to laugh.

I got to see firsthand the effects of humor on people's well-being and what an effective stress reliever it is. People would come up to me after shows and tell me how much they needed to laugh, how much *better* they felt and how they don't laugh enough in their daily lives. They would say that for the duration of the show, they were able to forget all of their problems and concerns.

I've been fascinated with the healing effects of laughter and its positive effect on our well-being ever since. It turns out there is a wealth of empirical evidence that supports this notion. Laughter reduces the levels of stress hormones which are linked to everything from heart disease to obesity. It is a tremendous tool for relieving our stress and helps restore balance to our mind, body, and spirit. Plus it's fun, it's free, and it just feels good!

STRESS STRATEGY
Find the Humor in Everyday Life

It's undisputed that laughter is good for you, yet in our society, it's viewed as silly, frivolous and unnecessary. Think of all the places you can't laugh: You can't laugh in a business meeting, you can't laugh at a funeral, you can't laugh in Walmart. Well, you *can*, but not when you're by yourself. Trust me, I've tried it. They'll send the greeter over to gum you to death and it's not pretty!

Unintentional Humor: "That's not funny!" *Oh, yes it is!*

There is the potential for humor everywhere. Often, people are the funniest when they aren't trying to be. Our job is to be ever vigilant, keep our humor antennae up, and enjoy the funny stuff that is flying all around us. You don't have to look very far. It's probably as close as your immediate family.

My younger sister, Cindy, has a habit of mixing up adages and common phrases. I laugh like crazy (on the inside), but I never correct her. I don't want her to quit doing it and thus dry up a bottomless well of amusement for me. Here are a few Cindyisms:

- "She's just not the sharpest *tool in the sky.*"

- "Seriously, leopards don't change their *stripes.*"

- One day, we were playing online Scrabble and she said, "Man I got NOTHING! I am *up a pole* without a paddle." I was drinking a Diet Coke and it almost came out of my nose.

- A few months ago, I was telling Cindy that I was thinking about getting a snow blower. I was getting tired of shoveling my driveway. She was most supportive. She said, "Kay, get one! *At your age*, you don't need to be out there shoveling snow. You've got enough *eggs in the fire!*"

MUSING

Cindy is six years younger than I am. Her new favorite way to preface just about everything she says to me is with that ominous warning, "at your age." I suppose I could get offended, but I'm really too old to care, and at my age, I can't be stressing over this stuff. Six years ago, I probably would've been offended, back when I was "young" like my sister. Lucky for her "old" will always remain an elusive concept, always six years out of reach.

No one laughs louder at the Cindy-isms than my other sister Carol. But, she is the source of many Carol-isms. Sometimes, she asks polite questions, not really caring about the question or the answer.

I live sixty miles south of Columbus, Ohio, and I was telling Carol that I had a flight out of there in the morning. I could tell by the blank look in her eyes that I had lost her interest. (She was also doing that weird thing people do when you are boring them and they are stifling a yawn. Their nostrils flare and their chin quivers. They look like a cross between a rabbit and a gopher.)

So, even though she found me to be mind-numbingly dull, to be polite she asked, "Are you going to *drive* to Columbus?" I simply can't let a question like that just lie there or answer with a simple "yes."

I replied, "No. The plane is going to swing by my house and pick me up. I know! I can't believe it either! It costs a little extra, but it's so much easier than going through airport security. The neighbors complain about the noise and the plane taking out their shrubs, but it's still worth it."

I couldn't help but cackle at my clever response. I laughed even more when the blank look on her face was replaced with scorn and she looked like a *perturbed* rabbit/gopher.

"You know what they say . . ."

You hear all kinds of unintentional humor out in the world if you keep your ears peeled. (That is an expression I never fully understood. You *peel* potatoes. I'm not sure how to *peel* your ears, but it sounds painful.)

The really good adages always start with, "You know what they say," such as, "You know what they say: 'One man's roof is another man's ceiling.'"

[Insert cocked head and confused expression here.]

Here are a few *actual* adage mix-ups that I've heard lately (seriously, you can't make this stuff up):

- "I just love springtime when the *Mongolia* trees are blooming!"

- "My son gets that from me. It's *generics*."

- "That *bird* won't hunt."

- "It's six to one and half a dozen to *a mother*."

People. People! Good thing they're amusing. It helps offset how annoying they can be.

Running Jokes

I love running jokes. They can go on for years. I've had one with my sister Cindy that has gone on for over thirty years.

When I got out of college, I lived at home for a year. Cindy was in high school at the time. We were having a fight and I had to walk through her bedroom to get to mine. I was carrying my laundry basket and one of those pink dryer sheets fell out onto her floor. I left it lying there as I entered my room and slammed the door.

She was upset to start with, but this made her even madder. (I don't say "angrier" because "madder" is more accurate. She was *crazy mad*.) She picked up the dryer sheet, opened my door and attempted to throw it into my room. It merely fluttered to the floor. Her frustration escalated as she put everything she had into trying to get it into my room. I was doubled over with laughter watching her, red-faced, attempting to put that dryer sheet in my possession. Since she was so intent on making sure I had it, this motivated me to get it back to her.

Later, I hid it in her room.

Fast-forward to today. That dryer sheet has gone back and forth between the two of us for over thirty years. The fun of the game has been to see how creatively we can get it back to each other. She is the unofficial winner because one time, she had a waitress serve it to me. (Good one!)

As of this writing, there is a pink dryer sheet hidden in my sister's car, tucked inside the owner's manual. I'm not saying she *never* reads her owner's manual, but let's just say it could be years before she finds that dryer sheet.

Tupperware

If you think about it, some of the smallest things in life are interesting or amusing. Take a ubiquitous item like Tupperware. Do you realize it is practically indestructible? Seriously, you can't kill it. The only things that would survive a nuclear holocaust are cockroaches, Tupperware, and Donald Trump's hair. Makes you wonder why they don't make airplanes out of the stuff (Tupperware, not Donald Trump's hair). I admit it would be kind of weird for the pilot to have to "burp" the plane before takeoff.

Tupperware parties have gone by the wayside only to be replaced by jewelry, kitchen utensils, and naughty lingerie parties. (Not at the same time. But *that* would be an interesting party if you think about it!)

I find it sad that Tupperware parties have become extinct because I always found them to be hugely entertaining. The Tupperware dealers actually used the word "exciting" to describe the items. Don't get me wrong, I like a good plastic storage product as much as the next person, but I've always failed to get *excited* over it.

Today, you can find Tupperware at county fairs, craft shows, or other similar events. It now comes in so many varieties and specific uses that you actually have to tell the dealer *what* you'll be storing in it before they can help you. I'm tempted to have some fun with it: "What will I be storing in it? My rather extensive collection of celebrity gallstones." With my luck, she wouldn't be shocked but rather get *excited* that they just came out with a bowl precisely for that. And it comes in three *exciting* new colors.

Despite my chiding, I do believe that Tupperware is great stuff. So is Pampered Chef, the line of kitchen utensils. But if I were really being pampered, I wouldn't be cooking at all, but rather being cooked *for*. So to me, the phrase "pampered chef" is an oxymoron. I mean think about it.

....

Look at the "little" things all around you and see if you can look at them with fresh, new eyes. There is more humor in them than you might realize.

Point to Ponder

- Have you laughed today?

Lighten Up!

Obviously I'm a big proponent of humor, but I don't think that it is a cure-all. Used improperly, it can be used as an escape and create more problems than it helps solve. People can actually hide behind humor as a way to avoid addressing troubles in their lives.

Humor doesn't solve our problems, but it helps us reframe them. It relaxes us and puts us in a position to tackle our challenges from a centered place rather than from a fearful, anxious place. We can then stand back from the issues with a clearer view of the solutions.

Keeping a sense of humor also makes us more productive. People accomplish more when they are light-hearted and relaxed than they do when they are tense, uptight and nervous. After all, the song is called,

"Whistle While You Work," not "Tremble With Anxiety While You Muddle through the Day."

Good Humor

It's a generally accepted humor principle that it's bad form to make fun of something that someone can't change. Theoretically, a person can change being a jerk. Being three-feet tall, not so much, (stilettos aside). A person with an ounce of sensitivity can tell if a joke is at someone else's expense and causing that person pain or discomfort.

The rule of thumb is the same as for when we are debating on whether or not to eat something in the refrigerator that is likely past its prime: "When in doubt, don't!" Unless of course you enjoy being a jerk. I'm just saying.

The Art of Laughing on the Inside

Not everything that we find humorous needs to be voiced aloud. However, I think that what we find funny in the walls of our own minds is perfectly acceptable, no matter how dark or unfunny someone else might think it is. I call it the "Art of Laughing on the Inside."

We live in a civilized society and it's not really productive, nice, or smart to go around verbalizing all of our thoughts. It's actually a pretty good way to get yourself smacked from time to time. (However, if you *like* being thumped on then chat away. I do wonder if your interests may be beyond the scope of this book. I'm not judging, I'm just saying.) But for the rest of us who would rather not be pummelled on a regular basis, it is usually wise to *not* give a voice to all of our thoughts.

However, no one ever has to know what goes on inside our own minds. There's a nonstop party going on inside my head all the time! Whatever we need to think or feel to maintain the sanctity of our sanity is perfectly acceptable. Inside our hearts and minds are the last vestiges of total freedom. Let's exercise our free will and enjoy an active inner sanctuary.

The Burrito Blues

Sometimes, entire comedy show audiences will "laugh on the inside." I learned this the hard way. I've been asked, "What's the worst time you ever bombed on the comedy stage?" ("Bombing" means that the people didn't laugh and it was painfully and publicly obvious to everyone present that you tried and failed.)

Wow, where to start. There have been so many. I started doing stand-up comedy in 1984 and have certainly taken many trips to Bombsville, especially when I was touring nationally. There wasn't a comedy club, roadside bar, or chicken coop where I wouldn't play. It was that or not eat, or—God forbid—go back to Dysfunction Junction, another company on the verge of bankruptcy. [Shudder]

One particular night stands out because it was a turning point for me. It was in Sedalia, Missouri circa 1987. I was the only comedian on the bill and after an excruciatingly poor response from the audience, I left the club in search of something to eat.

It was late at night in a small town and the only place open was a service station with a convenience store. I hadn't eaten all day, so I figured a gas station burrito was better than nothing. Or with any luck, they'd have some rotisserie hot dogs that had been there for less than twenty-four hours. I knew I could always scrape off the outer layer of e-coli. I had done it many times before and hadn't died yet. Besides, mustard masks a multitude of meat mediocrity. (Say *that* three times fast! No, seriously. Do it. I'll wait.)

Anyway, I pulled into the parking lot of the convenience store and saw four of the people from the audience in the store. So, I backed up, hid my car in the shadows and waited for them to leave. There I was, hunkered down in my car, too ashamed and embarrassed to go into the store and face them. I then got that crazy mix of emotions where you don't know whether to laugh or cry, so you do both. I'd bombed before but I had never felt that I had hit rock bottom like I did that night.

I questioned my career path and my very existence. I thought I was invisible there in the shadows, alternately sobbing and laughing like a drunken hyena. But when the people came out of the store, one of them spotted my car with the Ohio license plates. And I guess I wasn't as hunkered down as I thought I was because one of them said, "Hey, it's the comedian!"

To my horror, they started walking towards my car. My first instinct was to fire up the engine and run them over. Instead, I steeled my defenses and was ready to tell them what they could do with their crummy little town, their gas station burritos, their opinions, and anything else I could think of. As they got close, one of them said, "Hey, you did a great job tonight. Thanks a lot."

"Yeah," another one echoed, "we come to comedy night every week and you were the best we've seen."

Evidently there was a standard for the room that I wasn't aware of. These were people who had perfected the "Art of Laughing on the Inside." If you got "miles of smiles" from them, you were doing quite well. Unfortunately, the room was too dark for me to see their smiles. Indeed, it was too quiet for me to realize there were people even *in* the room.

What made this event a turning point for me was that I decided then and there that if the audience didn't laugh that I'd never take it personally again. For all I knew, people were actually enjoying themselves out there in the darkness. I also vowed to never let an audience define me in such a way as to make me question myself like that. Sure my job was to make them laugh, but it wasn't the End of the World if they didn't. It didn't kill me. I had a better chance of dying from the burrito.

From that point on, when I had a bad show—and believe me, there were many—I tried to see if there was anything to be learned from the experience, then let it go. I also realized that it's not possible to please everybody. I've attempted to carry these lessons into other areas of my life as well. I'm proud to report that I can now walk into any all-night convenience store in the country with my head held high. That's progress, my friends.

....

I came to realize that the things I stress about aren't as life or death as I sometimes make them out to be. A little bit of perspective goes a long way.

Points to Ponder

- Where could you find more humor in your life?
- Are the issues that you're stressing over really a matter of life or death?

CHAPTER TWO

....

The Funny Thing About Modern Life

*Stress is the trash of modern life—we all generate it
but if you don't dispose of it properly,
it will pile up and overtake your life.*

—Terri Guillemets (1973)

*I*n these modern times, we have the stress of technology. In many ways, it makes our life easier but more and more, we find ourselves talking to machines instead of people. We live in the land of "push this for that and that for this." At times, it feels like it just might push us over the edge!

Do You Scan With U-Scan?

Sometimes I like to scan my grocery items myself. I then encounter the stress of trying to please the U-Scan machine. "She" starts off really nice then gets progressively bossier and more aggravated:

> Welcome valued customer! Please scan your club card now. If you don't *have* a club card, please be prepared to pay five dollars for a can of corn. No, I'm not kidding. Just try me. Now scan your first item and place it in the bag. I haven't got all day.

Now that sounds easy enough. But it all goes downhill from there. You do as you're told: you scan the item and put it in the bag. It sounds like a simple task, but more often than not, you have displeased the machine. You can practically hear the irritation in her voice:

"Please place the item in the bag. *IN THE BAG!*"

So, you try to rescan the item and fail miserably. This *really* puts her wires in a twist. She gives you a heavy sigh and then laments, "Please wait for cashier's assistance. You are too stupid for words. I've got a better idea. Reload your cart and go find a lane with a real cashier and leave this job to the paid professionals. Seriously, you're giving me a headache."

At least that's what it *sounds* like she is saying. I'm surprised *she* doesn't make little comments about your purchases: "Ice cream? What, are you kidding me? Have you stepped on the scales lately, Tubby?"

The U-Scan machine's not crazy about cash either. You rifle through your wallet looking for the freshest, crispest, least wrinkled bill in there. You can smooth down the corners, stretch it, lick it, stomp on it, sit on it, and iron it, but that machine is going to reject it at least once. When the dollar reemerges, it looks like it's sticking its tongue out at you! If you try the same bill again, it will threaten you with cashier's assistance. Heaven forbid you get out of there with any dignity. Then the machine turns into your mother: "Don't forget to take your cash, located below the receipt printer. Don't forget your umbrella, it might be raining out. Don't forget to give me grandchildren."

If the U-Scan lady gets too annoying, you can always go to a live cashier instead. Of course, you're going to have to deal with that thinly-veiled accusation, "Do you have anything in the bottom of your cart?" I always say, "Just the stuff I'm planning to steal." You can use that. Just be sure to say it with a big, charming grin so they don't take you seriously. You do NOT want to be strip-searched by the bag boy. Trust me on this

Self-Service Gas Stations

The gas pump machine is as bossy as the U-Scan lady. The commands are in writing, but the "tone" is still there: "Turn off your cell phone, don't top off your tank, and don't even *think* of driving off without paying. By the way, we're having a sale on HoHos."

You then have to answer a bunch of questions before they allow you the privilege of pumping your own gas: "Can you pay? Really? *How*? Cash, debit, or credit? Inside or outside? Do you want a receipt? Unleaded or Diesel? Boxers or briefs?"

But then your choices are "yes, no, or enter." It's easier to decipher the Da Vinci code. I'm guessing it's all part of the authorization test to see how badly you want their gas and what you are willing to do to get it.

If you swipe your credit card, it's usually too fast, too slow or turned the wrong way so you have to do it again.

They're probably just charging us twice.

As the interrogation continues, the whole process starts feeling like they are trying to discover if you are a communist: "Are you a Special Club Member? Have you ever *been* a Special Club Member? Do you *know* anyone who's a member? What do you know and when did you know it?"

Sometimes you have to wait for authorization. You know how there is always a room inside the convenience store for authorized personnel only? I figure that's where the authorization committee hunkers down. After much deliberation, they send out a representative to announce over the PA, "Pump six, it's your lucky day! After careful consideration and a three to two vote, we've decided to bestow upon you the honor of purchasing our over-priced gas."

For just a second, you feel kind of special, don't you? You look at all those other poor suckers still waiting for their verdict and you want to brag just a little, or break into song. Have you ever been turned down? It's mortifying!

"Pump three, we don't think so. We're going to need you to come to the window. And please walk with your hands on your head. It's apparent you can't be trusted."

You have to do that Walk of Shame to the window while everyone shakes their heads and averts their eyes in that mix of contempt and embarrassment.

Like all of that isn't enough, you go to wash your windshield and there's this dried up, ratty squeegee and no paper towels. It's pretty bad when you pay their ridiculously high gas prices, then have to spit-shine your own windshield and dry it with the tail of your shirt. I'm just saying.

I don't like paying at the cashier's window because I can never find my pump number. I say, "I'm the car over there" as I wave vaguely in the direction of four or five pumps. Would it kill them to make the pump numbers large and visible? Or is an eye test part of the authorization process?

"No, THAT one . . ."

You know you're in a bad neighborhood when the convenience store is locked up and you have to order what you want by pointing at the items through the bulletproof window.

"Yeah, give me a Diet Coke.

Not Coke Zero.

Not caffeine-free.

That one.
No, that one.
Not a bottle.
The can.
YES!
And gimme one of those donuts.
No, not that one, THAT one.
No, *next* to that one.
The other way.
Now down."

Meanwhile, a line is forming behind you and they're all glaring at you like you've got a hundred items in the express lane. Now you're even *more* stressed because you're also adding to other people's bad days. It's contagious!

GPS

Talk about bossy!
GPS: Go right
Me: Right?
GPS: You heard me.

Do we really need a machine in our cars sassing us? And I swear mine gets extra "attitude" when I go a different way and she starts shrieking, "Recalculating! Recalculating! You're killing me here!" Sheesh. Whine much?

I think my old boyfriend had a crush on his GPS lady. He even had a little pet name for her: "Gypsy." I'd be in the middle of a sentence while we were in his car and when she'd start talking, he'd shush me, "Shh!! She's talking!"

I'm not above admitting that I was a little jealous. I mean, he never let *me* give him directions. Maybe it was my imagination, but I swear one time when we got in his car, I heard her say, "Hey big boy. Have you missed me?"

Then she told *me* where to go, and not in a good way.

Credit/Debit Card Machines

I can never figure out if I'm supposed to swipe my card myself or give it to the cashier. It doesn't matter if the box is sitting right there, that's no indication that you are supposed to use it. More times than not, you go to swipe it and the cashier says, "No, no. Give it to *me*. The box doesn't work." But if you hand it to the cashier without swiping the box, she'll say, "No, no, like it says right there in *plain English*, swipe HERE." Then she swipes it *for* you. That really hurts. It's usually accompanied by an eye roll and a heavy sigh.

Want to have some fun with them? Pretend that you think "swipe" means "steal." Rip the box out of the counter and run out of the store with it. Explain to the greeter, "But she said to *SWIPE* it!" High five the people on the way out and laugh maniacally. You won't soon be forgotten plus you'll have your own private box to tote from store to store: "I'll be using my *own* machine today."

Indoor Outhouses

Public restrooms are stressful for the same reasons they have always been: they're restrooms you share with the general public! But, to add to the anxiety is the fact that many are high-tech now and when you walk in, you never know what to expect. They are either completely automated, completely manual or a mix of the two. It's a veritable minefield of technology.

Back in the old days, you would finish, and then flush the toilet with your foot. End of story. Nowadays, some of them are the kinds that have sensors that flush the toilet automatically. The problem is that they go off when you don't want them to, but refuse to when you *do* want them to.

According to my limited understanding, men and women part ways a bit on restroom protocol, so let me explain a little bit about our rituals. But hang with me guys. For I will answer this age-old question: "What takes women so long in the restroom?"

You can thank me later.

The Women's Room

Women enter the stall and immediately begin building a toilet paper fortress on the seat. (Well, you can't just sit right down, because everybody knows that's how you get pregnant.) So, after unloading a half a roll of paper on the seat and getting it just the way we want it, we turn around, our motion activates the sensor, it sucks all the toilet paper down and we have to start over! But, of course when we *want* the toilet to flush, no luck. We stand there doing the Macarena, trying to activate the sensor. We look everywhere for the "manual flush" button which is normally unmarked and well-hidden for reasons known only to the manufacturer. You'll usually find your face two inches from the toilet seat in your hunt for the elusive button. That's just nasty!

However, for no apparent reason, you get a "welcome flush" when you enter the stall. You want to thank the toilet. With that kind of enthusiastic greeting, you're half expecting a mai tai and a marching band.

How Dry I Am . . . or Am I?

Even the paper towel dispenser, the water and the soap are often automated. When they only offer an air dryer, there is usually this long-winded explanation posted as to why they do that. It always mentions their goal of protecting us from the disease caused by "paper towel litter" coupled with their deep concern for the environment. It says suspiciously little about the automation being a cost-saving measure for *them*. Shocking, I know. And really, have you ever been to a funeral where the person died of the dreaded "Paper Towel Litter Disease"?

And has anyone in the history of the universe ever gotten their hands completely dry using a hand dryer? We don't have that kind of time *or* patience. It's a quick pass under the dryer, and then we walk out holding our hands up like a surgeon that has just scrubbed in and opening doors with our elbows or rear ends. *Or* we wipe our hands on our pants. Nice.

Compounding the stress of the public restroom is that you never know from one restroom to the next what level of automation you will encounter. One time, I was doing the chicken dance while waving my hands under the faucet, trying to get the water to flow. This person next to me says, "Um, you just turn the handle." Then she looked at her friend, raised her eyebrows and did circles around her ear with her index finger, making the universal sign for "crazy." Who needs this?

Communal Commodes

Yes, women take a long time in the restroom. There are certain things in life you can count on:

1. The sun will rise in the morning.

2. Politicians will lie. (My dad used to say, "They *stretch the blanket*.")

3. There *will* be a line at the ladies room.

From what I understand, men all line up in a row with no partitions in between the urinals. It would take women even longer if we had no stalls. I can just see the commodes all lined up in a row, some women perched on their toilet paper fortresses, some hovering precariously over the seat:

"Hey, Sue! Just what *is* the secret to your Mississippi mud cake?"

"Butter!"

"Anybody have any paper? Pass it down! And write down that recipe, will you?"

"Nice shoes!"

We'd never get out of there.

MUSING

Back in the old days, gas station restrooms had cloth towels. Well, it was more like cloth "towel." It was one gigantic towel on an endless loop. Problem with this was that once you got to the end of the towel, they didn't bother to change it out and you'd end up wiping your hands on the same piece of towel that the previous fifteen patrons had used. They never really worked out their propensity to jam up either. Either way, you had little choice but to share it with all of those disease-ridden strangers (and they with you). Good times.

Adding to an already long ritual, some women take their used paper towel and spend ten minutes cleaning up the water spillage on the counter area, whether they splashed it there or not. Sometimes I purposely splash a little extra to give them more to do. They don't mind. They live for this. They don't even expect tips! It amazes me. I want them to come to my house and clean up *all* of my messes. I could keep them busy and content for days.

The Men's Room

Occasionally, women are forced to use the men's room. It goes like this: You are at a sporting event. There are four-hundred women in line. You look over and there is NO ONE at the men's room door. Just tumbleweeds rolling through. Cobwebs are beginning to form. So, you decide to bypass the line at the ladies room and use the men's room. First you get your girlfriend to guard the door for you. Heaven help the poor guy who wants to use the men's room during your "occupation." They encounter your girlfriend standing spread-eagled in the doorway like a guard at Fort Knox. Everything but the fatigues and the gun which are replaced by sheer audacity. Normally, the man will sheepishly say:

"Excuse me, but I think this is the *men's* room."

"Not right now, pal. I'm going to have to ask you to step back."

"But, the little icon is wearing pants."

"So is my girlfriend. They're Capri pants, but they still count. Sir, step back so no one gets hurt."

Anyway, this explains the age-old mystery as to why it takes women so long in the restroom. All of the above plus the fact that there's a buffet. (Okay, not really, but that's my pat reply when a man asks me why women take so long. That seems like the most understandable and forgivable excuse to them. It also makes them a bit jealous.)

....

Computers

Don't anthropomorphize computers—they hate it.

—Author Unknown

It takes one second to join a mailing list. But to unsubscribe you get the message, "Well, this could take awhile! You might still get communications from us for many months to come."

Or worse yet, they want a reason for *why* you don't want to hear from them anymore. You start feeling like you're breaking up with someone who just won't let go. You find yourself explaining, "Look it's not you, it's *me*. You're really a great website and I'm sure you'll find someone else. We can still be friends. Don't cry. You know I hate it when you cry."

It's pretty uncomfortable for all involved. Well, maybe not for the computer that won't let you go. It doesn't care.

And why is it when we enter our email address, they make us do it twice? Don't they trust us? Is our collective typing *that* bad?

Spam

There are two kinds of spam. One is a canned meat byproduct that comes surrounded by gelatinous goo. The other is unwanted email. Neither is especially desirable, but the emails are worse. SPAM the meat byproduct doesn't show up in your inbox, trying to sell you enhancement products for body parts you don't even have. Plus, it tastes good on a cracker.

My sister Carol got an email that claimed she was the sole heir to a Nigerian prince who had died and left her a fortune. They wanted all of her financial information (credit card numbers, for instance) to be able to "transfer the funds." She wrote back and asked that they direct-deposit her millions into the account of her favorite charity, then gave them a website. (Good one!)

Paying Bills

Paying bills . . . or as my sister Cindy and I call it, paying our "Williams." Cindy prefers to pay online, but I haven't gotten the hang of that, so I'm still writing the checks and putting them in the mail.

But here's my beef.

They make the process far more difficult than it needs to be. For example, why do they make you write the "Amount Enclosed"? It's right there on the check that we enclose with the bill. You feel like writing in the space provided, "Look on the *check*!" Then they want you to write the account number on the check. This is typically thirty to forty characters long. Who's got that kind of time? You want to write, "Look on the *bill*!"

I really don't know why they require all of this documentation and cross-referencing. Maybe accounts receivable departments are housed in extremely hot buildings forcing the clerks to open the mail in front of large fans. One can only assume that all of this wind separates the bills from the checks. The poor clerks probably spend most of their days on their hands and knees looking for matches. I hope these people are paid well. Or maybe they're paid on commission, depending on how many bills and checks they can reunite.

Ever wonder why they sometimes mysteriously claim they didn't receive your check? Oh they got it alright. It just got swept up in a wind tunnel and is probably in Montana by now.

The Stress of Too Many Choices

Have you gone shopping for sheets lately? It used to be easy. You just walked into a store and bought a set of sheets. Now they have all of these options. For example, many of them have "deep pockets." I guess that's in case we want to *sue* the sheets. And sheets have "thread count"; one-hundred, two-hundred, three-hundred. You think your job gets boring? How would you like to be a "Thread Counter"? Can you imagine?

"A hundred and *one*, a hundred and *two*. Huh? What'd you say? Oh, dude, you messed me up. Now I gotta start over: one, two, three. . . . "

Sheets even brag about being "no-iron." Thank heavens that will free up a couple of hours a week. I just hate it when friends call you to do stuff and you've got that big, fat pile of un-ironed sheets staring you in the face.

....

I really do appreciate many of the technological advances we enjoy. Although it would be nice to get through a day without being heckled, sassed and harassed by a machine, I have no desire to go back to the times when people did laundry with a washboard or hiked outside to use the outhouse. But with change comes stress and I think we have to keep technology in perspective. When a machine starts getting to us, we can maintain a sense of humor or simply turn it off. After all, we still control the switch no matter how smart the contraption thinks it is.

Points to Ponder

- What do you do to manage the stress of technology?
- Would you like more automation in your life or less?

CHAPTER THREE

....

The Funny Thing About
Day-to-Day Irritations

*Any idiot can face a crisis—it's this
day-to-day living that wears you out.*

—Anton Chekhov (1860–1904)

Our stress level is often determined by an accumulation of the "little things" that we all encounter in our daily lives. Let's take for example, a simple trip to Walmart. I know the cashiers are trying to be friendly, but I don't really like when they make little comments about your purchases. Oh, you know how it is: you stop in for a couple of items, like Midol, chocolate... a chainsaw. She winks and gets that conspiratorial grin on her face and whispers, "Big night, huh?"

Not a big deal in and of itself, but it's just one more thing in our day that makes us go, "Grr."

There's Something Fishy Going On Here

We do tend to stress over small things. I was in a restaurant and I overheard this woman complain to the waitress that her fish tasted "fishy." For heaven's sake, it's a fish! What's it supposed to taste like? Then I noticed the waitress actually rewarded this whining by knocking a few dollars off of her bill. I thought, "Well I am going to try this." I said, "Excuse me, but this pork chop tastes 'piggy.' And my friend's hamburger tastes a little on the 'beefy' side." She just glared at me and with her voice dripping in sarcasm said, "Oh, I'm *sorry*. I'll be sure to tell the cook."

No discount for me!

Cooking

I can get stressed just cooking. I admit I'm not the best cook. I bought a microwave oven and now I just burn stuff ten times faster. Talk about rice pilaf? To me, that's the stuff that sticks to the bottom of the pan. (Rice *peel*-off. Get it?)

Even making spaghetti can be a challenge. Well, the directions on the box say, "Cook 10–12 minutes." Which is it? Ten, eleven, or twelve? I don't want options.

I want to be *told*. And then it says in big bold letters, "DO NOT OVERCOOK!" like you're going to be arrested or something. Like the Pasta Posse is going to come bursting into your kitchen, "I'm Big Al Dente and we're taking you in, ma'am. Abuse of a noodle." You can't decide if you are more upset that they burst into your house without wiping their feet or that they called you "ma'am."

Especially if you're a dude!

....

There are potentially stressful situations everywhere. They are seemingly minor events that build up over the course of a day. It starts with the so-called "little things," and these little things add up. I call them "capillary cloggers." We tend to think that big, major events are what cause our diseases and illnesses, but they are usually just the straw that tips us over the edge from relative good health onto the hospital gurney. Let's look for the humor as we navigate through the rough waters of our daily lives.

Point to Ponder

- What are some "small things" that stress you out in your day-to-day life?

CHAPTER FOUR

....

The Funny Thing About Driving

Patience is something you admire in the driver behind you and scorn in the one ahead.

—Mac McCleary

There are so many anxieties that are inherent with driving that the topic could be a book in itself. Sharing the streets and highways with others is one of those unavoidable communal experiences for all of us except the agoraphobics who can't leave the house. We have to trust that there are rules that we all need to follow to ensure flow and safety on the roads.

Part of the problem is that we all secretly think we are great drivers and everyone else falls short. We call people who drive slower than us "morons" and people that drive faster than us "idiots." Nice. It's a wonder any of us ever get where we're going with this kind of animosity.

We further think that *we* can drive while eating, talking on the cell phone, changing clothes, shucking corn, chopping wood, and playing the saxophone, but that no one else is remotely capable of this level of multi-tasking.

And there is something about being surrounded by a half ton of steel and fiberglass and traveling at a high rate of speed that heightens people's bravery. I've never seen anyone turn around and give the middle finger to someone who has bumped them with a grocery cart. But you irritate someone on the highway and the "birds" are flying! It's the speed combined with the machine that incites the action.

You won't normally see the universal sign of disgust when you are side-by-side with someone at a red light, no matter how much you've ticked them off. It's likely they won't look at you at all, choosing instead to stew and simmer while looking straight ahead, avoiding eye contact at all cost.

Go Granny Go

Not all of the anxieties of driving have to do with other drivers. I used to weigh the penalty of getting a speeding ticket against the consequences of not getting where I needed to be on time. I finally learned to just leave earlier. What a revelation that was! Being in middle age, I can't bat my eyelashes at the young cops and get out of the citation:

Me: [Batting eyelashes] Are you sure you want to give me that ticket?

Young cop: Ma'am? Do you have something in your eye? You gonna be okay to drive? Is there some-one I can call, like a son? Grandson? *Great* grandson?

Me: Just give me that ticket you whippersnapper! I didn't think you gave tickets to pretty girls.

Young cop: We don't, ma'am. Sign here.

Ouch.

Jam While You're Jammed

Traffic jams are situations that always have the potential to push us to the breaking point. But they are perfect examples of how we still have choices in situations we don't choose. We can opt to sit and simmer, but guess what? We won't get there any faster. For that matter, knowing the cause of the jam won't get us there any faster either.

Some people *must* know. They will leave their cars and start walking forward, talking to other drivers along the way to ascertain the cause of the jam, fuming all the way. Your other choice is to relax and enjoy the downtime. Why waste your energy on situations you have no control over? Why put yourself into "fight or flight" mode when you are unable to fight *or* flee? Why not sing instead?

MUSING

Singing is a great remedy for stressful situations. It doesn't matter if you aren't a good singer (which is like driving; we all secretly think we're pretty good). Anything that increases blood flow and oxygen helps to release stress and restore balance, like singing, exercise, and making whoopee. So why not hit the blood–oxygen trifecta and do all three at once? (There's an image you'll have a hard time getting out of your head.)

Four-way Stops

Speaking of stress on the streets and highways, didn't there used to be *laws* surrounding four-way stops? When did the rule become, "Y'all just work it out amongst yourselves"? You pull up to a four-way stop with a group of complete strangers who are all looking at each other as if to say, "Who knows the law? Anybody? Do I go? Do you?"

Luckily, there is usually someone who appoints themselves the President of the Four-way Stop and they take charge: "Look people, here's how this is going down. I don't trust any of you, so I'll go last so that none of you clueless airheads will hit my car." Then they point at us, one at a time, "'You' go, then 'you,' then 'you.'"

And we give them a thank-you wave that is so big we almost get a rotator cuff injury. We can't help but think, "Thank God you were here to direct us! We'd be here for hours if not for your wisdom and guidance. Or worse, we would've all gone at once, causing a three-car pileup in the middle of the intersection!"

We're so grateful, we want to throw them a party or name our first born child after them.

Sarcasm aside, I suppose we really *should* feel gratitude for the control freaks that save us from our own demise. At the very least, they prevent us from sitting at a four-way stop for hours on end, inching forward and backward with three other confused, frustrated fellow drivers thinking, "Do I go? Do you? Anybody?"

We'd never get where we're going.

The Law

I do believe in being a good citizen and following the rules, but how can we really be expected to never break the law? There are over one million laws on the books. We can't possibly know them all, let alone be expected to keep them. Talk about stress! I probably break two laws before I even leave the driveway.

Sometimes I break the law on purpose, just to prove that "The Man" doesn't have control over me. Immature, I know, but it makes me feel good. I have to confess, I've got a bit of a rebel streak and a few lingering issues with authority figures that I haven't quite worked through.

Normally, I use two criteria to determine which law I'm going to break:

1. Is it a stupid law?

2. Can I break it and not get caught?

I do believe in personal responsibility and if I get caught, I cheerfully accept my punishment. (Okay, not "cheerfully," more like "grudgingly" but I accept it nonetheless. Like I have a *choice*.) Sometimes it's just fun to push the envelope. If it's 2:00 a.m. and I'm at a stoplight and there's not a *soul* around, there's a better than average chance that I'm going to amble on through that red light. I get to continue on my way a tad sooner, *plus* that little thrill of beating "The Man."

....

Driving on our nation's streets and highways is a test for even the sanest among us. But the stress management principles remain the same: find the humor, monitor your reactions, and keep a light heart.

One of the hardest aspects of life is determining what is within our control. The rest we just have to let go of and then try to enjoy the ride.

Point
to
Ponder

- What can you do about the stress of driving?

CHAPTER FIVE

....

The Funny Thing About the Good Old Days

If you're yearning for the good old days,
just turn off the air conditioning.

—Griff Niblack

Stress has always been with us. Yet from time to time, I get one of those email "forwards" outlining how good life was "back in the good old days." They will talk longingly about how simple life was:

> Back in the good old days, we all just played kick-the-can all day. We chewed Clove gum and ate little wax Coke bottles filled with colored sugar water. Mmm! Why, our moms would take chicken out of the freezer and lay

it out on the counter for *days* [which might account for the unusual number of stomach aches that I had as a kid]. Why, we all ate lead paint and there's nothing wrong with any of *us*!

THAT is certainly debatable!

These emails lampoon all of the silly rules applied to people today and how "over-regulated" we are. In some ways, I think life *was* better and simpler, but in other ways, I think life is easier and more preferable today.

Take a trip back in time with me.

Television

Stress is nothing new, even though we have stressors today that we didn't have growing up. If you were raised in the 1950s or '60s, you know that we didn't have the technology that we have today.

We didn't even have remote controls for our television sets. In our family, the remote control was *me*: "Kay, get up and change the channel." To do this, I actually had to *get up out of the chair.* After I did that, I had to *walk across the room.* The horror!

Changing the channel wasn't that easy to do because three days after you bought the television, the dial would break and you'd have to use pliers to change it.

There were only three television stations, so you'd have to keep going around and around until everyone settled on what they wanted to watch. (Yes, the family all shared one television!)

Occasionally, someone would get the boneheaded idea to try to get one of the UHF stations. This dial had a thousand channels but you couldn't get any of them. It didn't stop us from trying.

[Clickclickclickclick] "Wait! I see a picture! Never mind, it's just snow. Keep clicking. [Clickclickclickclick-clickclickclick] Okay, okay, just go back to Channel 9."

I don't think my dad ever touched a television dial in his entire life. He would sit and wait until someone entered the room, then tell *them* to change the channel. What if it was hours and hours before someone came in? I often wondered how long he would sit and watch a station he wasn't interested in, just to keep from having to *get up out of the chair* and *walk across the room*. No one was happier than my dad when they finally came out with remote controls. He called it the "turner-onner-offer" and it was one of his most cherished possessions.

Back in the day, we didn't have cable television because there was no such thing. If your reception wasn't any good, you used an antenna called "rabbit ears." And if that didn't work, you'd wrap them in aluminum foil. I guess that was to seal in the freshness.

Sometimes you couldn't get a picture at all, even with the three regular channels. Just lots and lots of snow. Sometimes you sat and stared at the television anyway, but you were forced to use your imagination as to what you were seeing. Good times.

Automobiles

Automobiles and laws were completely different then. For one thing, we no longer call them "automobiles" favoring the monosyllabic "cars." Automobiles didn't have seat belts. We didn't need them: we had Mom's "bionic arm" reaching across the seat to keep us intact. My mother did that until I was forty-two years old. I finally had to tell her, "Mom, please take your hand off my chest. It's just creepy."

A child's favorite way to ride in the car was to lie across the back windshield. That would get you arrested today. I can also remember riding in the back of Dad's pickup truck. That's a big no-no today, too. My mom worried if it was safe. I can remember Dad saying, "Mom," (which I never understood. Wouldn't that make him my brother? Ew!) Anyway, he'd say, "Mom, I believe I'll take these four kids for the afternoon in the back of the pickup truck."

Mom would fret, "I don't know if that's all that safe."

"Okay, I'll leave them here with you."

"No, no! Y'all hold tight now!"

Apparently, the horror of spending the afternoon with the four of us outweighed the fear of her offspring being catapulted from the bed of a moving vehicle.

Automobiles didn't have air bags. The only thing that happened upon collision was that the glove compartment would fly open and thousands of S&H Green Stamps would come fluttering out.

When my napkin stash starts getting low, I actually go *inside* McDonald's instead of the drive-thru to replenish. I used to ask the drive-thru attendants for extra napkins, but they're so stingy, they'll usually only give you one or two. "Here you go!" I'm thinking, "Gee thanks, Captain Generosity. This will last me for about a minute and a half."

MUSING

Do they even call it a "glove compartment" anymore? To me, it ought to be called a "McDonald's napkin compartment." If you're like me, you've handed the cop a McDonald's napkin instead of your registration card more than once. I've actually done it on purpose, hoping the officer will use it to wipe the smirk off his face.

Riding With Mom and Dad

When we were in the car with Dad and we'd get frisky, he would give us a "warning shot," "If I have to pull this car over . . . ."

With Mom, there was no warning shot. She used to drive us to church every Sunday. Dad didn't go because he was a "C&E": Christmas and Easter. When we saw our dad wearing a suit, we knew that it was because of one of the following:

1. It was Christmas.

2. It was Easter.

3. Somebody died.

Looking back, I think I now understand why Dad opted out of going to church. Being a teacher and a father it was the only three hours a week he could spend kid-free. I can just "see" Dad dancing around the empty house, wearing nothing but boxer shorts and black socks singing, "I'm free! I'm free!"

So, every Sunday, Mom dutifully took the four of us kids and an elderly woman to church. The trip was seventeen miles each way and we had to travel on a winding, hilly road. I was sick every Sunday because:

1. I was crammed in the backseat with my three siblings. (With our Sunday finery on, we weren't allowed our usual spot in the back windshield.)

2. The car had no air conditioning.

3. The Salmonella Chicken Casserole from the night before was weighing on my stomach and gag reflex.

I'm sure it comes as no surprise that we would get "frisky."

Mom had no patience for this and there was no warning shot like Dad would give us. She wouldn't even stop the car. She would yell, "Hold your heads up here!"

And we would do it!

The four of us would all lean forward and without taking her left hand off the steering wheel or her eyes off the road, Mom would reach back with her right hand and smack whatever heads she could reach. She would run her hand back and forth across our four heads like she was playing a xylophone. Sometimes, my brother would put his hands around my throat and put *my* head up there, front and center, so I was the only one who would get smacked. Life is so unfair.

MUSING

After telling this anecdote in a presentation, a woman approached me to share her story. When she was growing up, her family had a station wagon and the kids would ride in the very back of the car. Their mom couldn't reach the kids to smack them, so she taped a fly swatter to a yardstick to extend her reach. THAT is ingenuity!

Oh, Brother!

My brother, Glenn, is four years older than I am and when we were kids, he used to pound on me like I was his own private punching bag. There were times he would hit me so long and so hard on one arm that I'd be begging him to hit me on the *other arm*. That's just sick. I wouldn't even be doing *anything*. [Insert feigned innocent expression here.]

One time, I cleaned his room from top to bottom. Of course, I had to go through *everything*. [Insert evil cackle here.] I even washed his record albums—with an S.O.S. pad—then laid them out in the sun to dry. You can imagine the warped, garbled version of "'Scuse me while I kiss the sky" by the time the water and sun got done with it. Glenn ran whining to our mother, "Mom! Kay took Jimi Hendrix out back and messed him all up!"

Of course, my mom had no idea who Jimi Hendrix was. She said, "Kay, go down to Jimi Hendrix's house and apologize to him!"

"She can't, Mom. He's DEAD!"

"Kay, quit killin' your brother's friends."

Sometimes I don't think Mom was really listening. I mean really.

My only defense against my brother's relentless torment was passive-aggressive psychological torture. I'd glare at my brother and say, barely above a whisper, "You've got to sleep *sometime*."

Here I am with Glenn circa 1961. (I'm the one in the dress. He's the one in the goober-looking saddle shoes and the facial expression that looks like he eats little sisters for breakfast. That's because he *did*.) Look at me! I look like I was adopted from a third world country. "He beats me and eats all my food!" Lord, look at my legs. You could floss your teeth with those things! Seriously.

Party Lines

We had one phone; it was black and tethered to the wall. We also had to share the telephone line with all of our neighbors. This was incorrectly called a "party line" because it was anything but a party. You always had that one nosy neighbor. You could hear her click on:

"Ethyl, I can hear you breathing."

"No I'm not."

Famous Blondes

To fully contrast yesterday with today, just look at who is famous. Back in the day, we had Debbie Reynolds and Doris Day. Today, we have Paris Hilton. She is famous and no one even knows why. But I know. Obviously, it's because of her name. Her first name is "Paris" like the exotic city in France. Her last name is "Hilton" as in the upscale hotel chain. Let's face it; we'd have never heard of her if her name was "Boise Budgetel." Or how about poor little "Cleveland Motel 6"? She's wallowing in obscurity somewhere in Northern Ohio. Nobody cares about *her* dalliances and she'll even leave the light on for us!

••••••••••••••••••••••••••••••••••••

I suppose that the debate will rage on as to whether we have evolved and improved, or whether life was better "back in the day" in contrast with our current treacherous downward spiral. Every generation thinks they are better than the one before. And every group looks back on their early years longingly and with fondness. I tend to think that the more things change, the more they remain the same. I think this quote best exemplifies that idea:

Children today are tyrants. They contradict their parents, gobble their food, and tyrannize their teachers.

—Socrates (470 BC–399 BC)

CHAPTER SIX

The Funny Thing About
Womanhood

**To by-pass this estrogen-infused
chapter, please skip ahead
to the next one.**

Don't say you weren't warned!

*But if you hang around, you might learn something
(or at least find amusement in how silly we can be).*

Let's just dive right in, shall we?

The G-Y-N

Going to the gynecologist has its own unique set of stressors. First of all, we actually take the time to root through our chest-of-drawers and pick out our best underwear. Why? It's not like anyone is going to see them. Because once we get into the exam room, we take off all of our clothes as instructed and then we HIDE the underwear. Lord knows we don't want them seeing anything *personal*.

We then put on that lovely paper outfit they issue to us, then perch on the edge of the examination table and wait. We will tuck that "skirt" under and pull the cape shut, doing everything but taping, stapling and padlocking it. Then, if we look over and see a bra strap hanging out from under our clothes, we will get off the table, go over and *tuck it under*. We sure don't want them knowing we wear one of *those*.

My advice to women everywhere: don't look at your chart! I made the mistake of looking at mine when the nurse laid it open. I noticed a "sketch" of something that looked suspiciously like a female body part. A really bad, skewed version of a female body part. It could have just as easily been a map of Georgia. I said, "What is that?"

She said, "Oh, that's a drawing the doctor did of you."

WHAT?

I always wondered what he was *really* doing during the exam. You're lying flat on your back with your feet up in stirrups. They strategically place that paper "skirt" across your legs so that you can't see the doctor. Now that I've seen his "artwork," I have this image of him down there with an easel and paint pallet, wearing a beret and sketching me like some kind of Vincent Van Cervix or PAP-casso.

I also noticed on the chart that there were two arrows pointing at the picture of me. He needs a map? How about a GPS?

"Turn right."

"Right?"

"You heard me."

What's he going to do next time to find his way? Drop bread crumbs?

The nurse informed me that the arrows were not a navigational tool, but were there to point out an "issue" of mine. Seems the doctor had discovered "something of concern" during my last visit and wanted to be reminded of it. Oh, THAT'S comforting. I suppose it's less creepy than the thought of him drawing me for one of his art school projects.

I might also suggest that while you are in the gynecologist's examination room that you don't ever look at the "tools." I made that mistake once. They line them all up on that unassuming little paper towel and, let me tell you, Black & Decker has *nothing* on these people! I found myself thinking, "Are we going to have an exam here or build a dog house?!"

Stages of a Woman's Life

You can tell what stage of womanhood you're in by what other people call you. Trust me on this. If you have any doubts, the world will let you know.

When you're a little girl, people call you "sweetie." Then you move into your teens and you're addressed as "young lady." When you reach your twenties and thirties they call you "miss." Before you know it the day comes when you're called "ma'am" for the first time. *That* is eye-opening. It's a rite of passage that serves as a notification that you have now arrived in middle age! You can no longer lull yourself into the illusion that the changes you are seeing in the mirror are simply due to "bad lighting."

If you live long enough, you go full circle and become "sweetie" again. Welcome to old age. Or they think it's uproariously funny to call you "young lady" as in, "Hey *young lady*, can I bring you some more beets?" I can hardly wait to get to old age. The smart aleck retorts are lining up in my mind like planes on a tarmac. Bring it on.

Speaking of planes, I got a premature "sweetie" on a flight recently and I didn't take it kindly. No one would dispute that since I'm over fifty years old, I am solidly in middle age. I accept that my "miss" days are behind me, but I'm nowhere near ready for "sweetie."

I was seated in the exit row and there are responsibilities that come with sitting in these seats. You have a "job" of sorts. If something goes awry—God forbid—it's your job to remove the emergency door, toss it out and help the other passengers escape the plane. You get extra legroom and they get an extra non-paid employee.

This young flight attendant leaned down, got her face about two inches from mine and said (loudly, like I was deaf), "*Sweetie?* That door weighs about forty pounds. Will you be able to lift it to throw it out?" [Fume] What I *wanted* to say was, "How about I throw *you* out the door?" but in this touchy climate, you don't dare sass the flight attendants. You'll find yourself being thrown from a plane at 10,000 feet and that *will* mess up your whole day, not to mention your makeup. Instead, I said, "Yes *ma'am*, I can!" From the look on her face, I'm pretty sure it was her first "ma'am." She scurried away, no doubt to find a mirror to search for gray hairs.

Adolescence

I remember when I became a "young lady"; when I had my first period. Like you could ever forget that kind of thing. I was horrified and Mom was delighted! I heard her on the phone with my aunt Betty:

"Kay just became a YOUNG LADY!"

I thought, "Sheesh, Mom why don't you hire a sky writer and just broadcast it to the whole world?!"

"Kay, come talk to Aunt Betty."

"I don't want to talk to Aunt Betty! . . . Hi Aunt Betty . . . I really don't think '*congratulations*' are in order . . . No, I don't want a party!"

Back in the old days the "equipment" was a lot different than what they offer today. Today, you've got minis, maxis, overnights, adhesives, dots, light days, scented, unscented, leaded, and unleaded; the choices are endless! Back then you had pads, metal belts and rivets. If you had all that gear on today, you'd never make it through airport security! I can see them waving their little wand all over you, "What on earth do you have *on*?" Okay, I exaggerated about the "rivets," but those belts were for real. Technically, they were called "*sanitary* belts." I always wondered, "Does this mean they are *clean*? I certainly hope so!"

The belts weren't very effective. By the time you got to school, the pad was somewhere up around your shoulder blades. (By the way, I do realize that some of the younger readers will have no idea what this "belt" is that I'm talking about. I suggest you ask a middle-aged female relative to explain it to you. Just don't call her "sweetie.")

Worse than the belt were safety pins. They were fine until one of them inadvertently snapped open. You would quickly hobble to the closest ladies room and that could be one painful walk!

Mom decided this was also the time to start shaving my legs, so along with the pads and belt she handed me a razor. Not one of those cute, little pink disposable razors like they have today. This was a double-edged samurai sword.

So I went in the bathroom and started hacking away. By the time I got done, our bathroom looked like the bloody shower scene from the movie *Psycho*. I had so many little pieces of toilet paper on my legs you could play connect-a-dot. Again, younger readers, ask about the hair-removal weaponry used "back in the day." If we used that sort of thing today, we'd likely be required to have it registered as a lethal weapon.

To dispose of the razor blade, there was a little slot in the back of the medicine cabinet. I wondered why it never filled up. I imagined there was some kind of razor fairy that came by in the night and removed the used blades. Or the slot was connected to some giant razor blade landfill somewhere. Apparently, we were "green" before green was cool.

MENOPAUSE: "The Big M," "Aunt Minnie"

At the age of fifty-five, I do get those occasional menopause moments where things slip my mind. I tend to think it's not because of "age" but rather the fact that my mental library gets more and more overloaded as time goes on. There's more knowledge and information than I've ever had before. Ironically, the more I know, the more I realize how little I really know. They call this "wisdom." Go figure.

By the way, I looked up "menopause" to make sure I spelled it correctly. It's pronounced "minnow paws," like a small fish with hands. I found this definition: "Men-o-pause: the time in a woman's life when menstruation diminishes and ceases, usually between the ages of forty-five and fifty."

That's it? *"Diminishes and ceases?"* This definition sounds like the gentle landing of a hot air balloon. Oh, there's hot air going on alright, but there's nothing easy and breezy about it! As a card-carrying member of the "Aunt Minnie Club," I can testify that there is much more going on than simply "diminishment and cessation."

(For you younger women, be forewarned that PMS is just dress rehearsal for "The Big M.")

A few years ago, my gynecologist suggested that *at my age*, I should get a blood test to see if I was in menopause. I said, "You really need a blood test? How about we save the needle and I'll just send you a gallon of the sweat that I wring from my bed sheets each morning!"

All this sweating and STILL the weight gain. It defies the laws of physics. "They" say universal laws are immutable, but I'm starting to have my doubts. My body defies the laws of everything except gravity.

Menopause: thinning bones, memory loss, night sweats, hot flashes. And those are the *upsides*!

The Pressure to Look Good

Women are bombarded with advertising and the message is that we aren't young/thin/pretty enough. Take for example the television show, *Extreme Makeover*. I could never watch that show. It's not because I couldn't bear to watch those plastic surgeries. It's because I'd likely find out there are fifty things wrong with me that I didn't even know about. And they can fix them! Like I don't have enough to obsess over as it is.

My friend is considering getting liposuction. I told her that I heard it's pretty painful. She said, "Not as painful as looking at myself naked in the mirror every day!"

I know this lady who got braces on her teeth at the age of forty. She said her dentist said her teeth are crooked and she could benefit from braces. And since she's been going to him for twenty years, she trusts his opinion. I said, "You've been going to him for twenty years and he just now *noticed*?"

I have to say, her teeth look great. But the crazy thing is, she also got breast augmentation and now no one notices her teeth. She's like, "Hey! My mouth is up here!"

Lethal Lashes

Just about the time I started feeling good about myself, I discovered that my eyelashes aren't "dangerously" long. I am amazed at how many types of mascara there are and how many ads there are to support all of them. Seems there are always "new and improved" versions.

Mascara is basically black paint. Yet, they keep coming up with more and more improvements:

"Extreme volume!"

"Ten times the length!"

How long and thick do our eyelashes have to be? Do we really need our eyelashes entering the room three minutes before we do? They're not going to stop until we all have black carpet samples hanging from our eyelids.

Toenail Squatters

And as if we don't have enough to stress about, now we find out that we have little creatures living under our toenails, partying, reproducing, and doing the conga. It wouldn't be so bad if they weren't so ugly! If I have to have creatures living under my toenails, why can't they at least be good looking? I'd say, "Party on, little Brads and Angelinas." Then I'd cover them with a lovely shade of nail polish and be done with it.

MUSING

There are marketing experts who spend their entire work-lives coming up with names for nail polish. My current favorite color is called, "My Chihuahua Bites!" My sister used to have one called, "I'm-Not-Your-Waitress Red." If I were a Nail Polish Namer, I'd name a color that described what nail polish is really for: "Use-this-so-you-don't-scare-small-children-with-your-horrific-big-toenail Pink." Just keepin' it real.

"Oh Mama!"

To survive all of the insanity that swirls around us, we simply have to laugh. It doesn't hurt if we can poke fun of ourselves as well. I find humor in my silly antics all the time.

The other day, I was shopping for clothes and I saw this really cute shirt. It was nice, long, and roomy—it would hide a multitude of flaws. I glanced at the tag and it was from a company called "Oh Mama!" I looked up and realized I was in the maternity department. AHH!!!!! I dropped that shirt like a two-dollar skillet and practically ran out of the store.

My first instinct was to run home and shower. Then I had to laugh at myself. What did I think was going to happen? From what I remember from seventh grade health class, no one ever made a baby by touching a maternity shirt. It would be my luck to be the first! One can't be too careful. I have no desire to have my story picked up by the AP newswire: "Fifty-five-year-old Woman Gets Preggers Touching a Shirt!"

Amazon Lady

I have felt just as silly wandering into the petite department by mistake. At nearly 5'11", that's the last place I need to be. It makes me feel like Dorothy from *The Wizard of Oz*, lost in Munchkinland. At any time, I figure one of the little people will say, "Are you lost, Amazon Lady? Follow the yellow brick road." Then,

I'd close my eyes and click my heels: "There's no place like the misses department."

When I make this faux pas, I feel like they're all pointing and laughing at me in their little munchkin voices, "Look at her! She thinks she's *small*! Teeeheee!"

Next time, I'll just step on them. That'll show 'em.

MUSING

Who had the bright idea to come up with a line of clothing for middle-aged women called "SAG Harbor"? I mean really.

CHAPTER SEVEN

....

The Funny Thing
About Childbirth

·

*T*he funny thing about childbirth is . . .

THE FUNNY THING ABOUT CHILDBIRTH

THE FUNNY THING ABOUT CHILDBIRTH

I think I've made my point.

CHAPTER EIGHT

···

The Funny Thing About Other People

A man's good breeding is the best security
against other people's ill manners.

—Lord Chesterfield (1694–1773)

One of the biggest causes of stress is Other People. And they are *everywhere*. The planet is literally infested with them. Seriously. Even Ted Kaczynski, the unabomber couldn't avoid Other People forever, though God knows he tried. Although he lived in the woods by himself, he just couldn't resist sending those mail bombs and rambling manifestos that eventually landed him in prison with—you guessed it—lots and lots of Other People. Oh, the irony of it all.

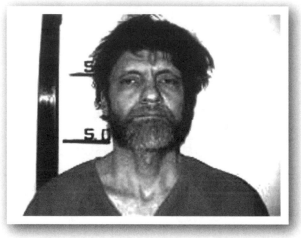

Ted Kaczynski

I bet he's thinking, "It's pretty obvious from this picture that the chicks dig me but sorry ladies, there's only so much Ted to go around."

MUSING

The FBI didn't catch the Unabomber until his brother ratted him out. Along the same theme, the father of the 2009 Nigerian Christmas Day "KnickerBomber" alerted authorities that his son was dangerous. LESSON: Before you decide to go on a bombing spree, be sure you are on good terms with your relatives. I'm just saying.

I can almost guarantee that where you find Other People, you find potentially volatile situations just waiting to happen. The Other People just can't help themselves. They will find ways to step on your feet, hit you with their shopping carts, break the rules, cough without covering their mouths, swerve into your lane, and wreak all kinds of havoc on your otherwise peaceful day. Now that I think about it, the Unabomber might have been onto something (not the bombing part, the living in the woods by himself part).

STRESS STRATEGY
Monitor your Reactions

Here's an eye-opener: although we can't often control what Other People say and do, we *can* control our reactions. HUH? My mom used to tell me, "Just ignore them." WHAT? How on earth do you go about doing that? That notion stymied me for years but I have to admit, Mom was right about this issue.

How we react to Other People's words and deeds is truly our only choice sometimes, and it *is* a choice. We *choose* our reactions to outside stressors that come in the form of people, places and things. The key is to monitor our thoughts and see if we can choose a new reaction that will decrease our level of anxiety.

The Art of the Snappy Comeback

I've learned that Other People can be downright rude. Hard to believe, I know. But it seems that I never have that snappy comeback handy when someone says something insulting. Does this happen to you, too? Driving away, I relive the conversation in my mind like a movie scene and think of all the clever and witty things that should've been part of my end of the script.

It's the "Art of the Snappy Comeback," and very few of us are masters at it. Mostly because people catch us off guard. And that's fine because our other option is to go around with our guard up to make sure we never have any "gotcha" moments. Quite frankly, that's exhausting. It's keeping ourselves in "fight" mode and will cause us more stress than the occasional unanswered insult.

New "Yawkers"

My years in New York City taught me to keep my mouth shut mostly because I was unsure of the consequences of mouthing off. You just never knew when you'd be the last straw to someone that was about ready to snap.

There is a common misconception that New Yorkers are rude. People from other parts get this idea when they visit the Big Apple and people whiz right past them on the street without a passing glance or even a "howdy." Truth is, if you live in that city and you stop for every person wanting directions, the time, a quarter, etc. you'd never get anywhere. So, you plaster on your "street face" and plow ahead.

I actually came to realize that a lot of New Yorkers are not rude as much as painfully blunt. I still think they could temper their bluntness with some tact, but I have to admit that for the most part, they were some of the most honest people I've ever known.

MUSING

I think back to when I first moved to New York City. I found that it was too expensive to continue the psychotherapy that I had started in Ohio. I heard about a program offered by a local university where they would take your case and a whole team of graduate students would analyze you under the watchful eyes of their instructors. And it was completely free! I thought this would be a dream come true.

I applied for the program and had a lengthy interview with a therapist to see if I qualified. After a few weeks, she called to tell me that I didn't get accepted into the program. At first I was disappointed, but then I thought, Well maybe I'm just too sane for them! So I asked her in a half-kidding way, "Oh. Was I just not screwed up enough for them?" In the blunt way that only a New Yorker can respond she said, "Oh no, you're plenty screwed up. You just weren't what they were looking for."

Ouch.

It wouldn't have killed her to throw in a little tact. Especially since I was so screwed up. I'm just saying.

Glasses

People can be rude, that's for sure. For example, I wear glasses and every now and then, I'll take off my glasses and someone will remark, "You know, you look a lot better without *those glasses*." That's so rude! Like I'd be wearing glass and metal hanging from my face if I had other viable options. I always squint at them and say, "I look better? You know, so do *you!*" Not understanding that they just insulted me they'll say something like, "Seriously, why don't you get Lasik surgery?"

"Why don't you get *lockjaw?*"

Okay, I don't actually *say* any of that. But, I say it in my head and it makes me feel better. I keep the "Art of Laughing on the Inside" alive and well in my world!

MUSING

One time someone actually suggested that I get "Lasix surgery." Lasix is a medication that helps people reduce the amount of fluid that their bodies are holding. In other words, it makes you pee. So, if I got Lasix surgery, I wouldn't be able to see any better but I'd be running to the bathroom all the time!

Did You Know?

The number one stressor in the American workplace is annoying coworkers. Oh, come on, you know there's one on every job. And if you can't think of one, it's probably *you.*

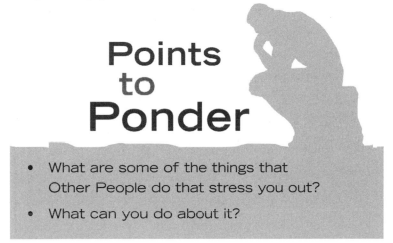

Points to Ponder

- What are some of the things that Other People do that stress you out?
- What can you do about it?

Create an Inner Oasis

Adopt the pace of nature: her secret is patience.

—Ralph Waldo Emerson (1803 1882)

An "inner oasis" is a frame of mind where we endeavor to maintain calm amidst the storm. You're engaged with what's going around you without becoming *submerged.* You *care* while keeping part of yourself on reserve.

A lot of people are experts at this; healthcare and hospice professionals, teachers, and funeral directors are good examples. People in these kinds of positions will burn out in a hurry if they don't learn to "care from a distance."

Those who have performed these jobs for a long time will tell you that creating an inner oasis is the key to long-term survival in these professions. This is not to say they have totally removed themselves emotionally and won't let anything touch them, only that they have learned that they must do what is necessary to protect themselves so that they can continue to provide these valuable services without getting burned out.

Humor is a huge part of their survival tool boxes, even when it has to be within the walls of their own minds. No one wants to see their surgeon or funeral director yukking it up during these most serious matters of life. On the other hand, it's immensely comforting when they are tuned into *our* need to release tension through humor and create a comfortable environment for this to occur.

DECIDE to Stress Less

Make it a conscious decision. Put it in the form of an affirmation that will work for you such as: "Today, I will let the 'little things' slide and focus on the big picture."; "I am creating a peaceful and productive day."; "Just for today, everyone can just kiss my [fill in body part]." Whatever works for you.

Points to Ponder

- Have you made a conscious decision to stress less?
- What can you do to create an inner oasis?

Uncommon Courtesy

Color me "old-fashioned," but I yearn for the good old days when you'd let someone pull out in front of you on the highway and you'd get a "thank you" wave. These have gotten to be few and far between and I want my kindness to be acknowledged!

Worse is when you hand someone money for a purchase and don't get a "thank you." These days, it's become common for people to hand you your change with, "Here ya go!" or "You're all set!" Where is my "thank you"? I used to find myself thanking *them*. Somebody has got to do some thanking in this transaction! I caught myself doing this and had to consciously vow to stop. I was actually showing gratitude to *them* for accepting my money.

Sometimes, I hand them my money and say, "Here ya go!" That trumps *their* "Here ya go!" and forces them to go to, "Have a nice day." One step closer to a "thank you." Maybe I'll start saying, "Here-ya-go-have-a-nice-day" really fast, thus preempting them and *forcing* them to go to all that's left, "Thank you." No, they'd find a way to bypass the "thank you" and go straight to, "You're all set."

Grr.

"Do you want your receipt in the bag?"

When was it decided that this was to be part of the exchange and not the "thank you"? To me, it's an odd question. I also think it's kind of personal. In a way, I don't think it's really any of their business where I want my receipt. Why don't they just hand it to me and let me stow it where I want? Why do they offer to put it in the bag *for* me? Do they think I'm incapable? If they're willing to put the receipt in the bag for me, would they be willing to put it anywhere I wanted it? Aren't they kind of setting themselves up for a potentially unpleasant situation? What if I turned around and offered up my backside, "I'd like it in my back pocket. Would you mind?" Or between my cheek and gums. Or stuffed inside my bra.

Be careful what you ask for retail people, that's all I'm saying. There ya go! Free advice and you don't even have to thank me. You're all set!

Volunteers, Not Victims

We often feel like victims when in fact we are volunteers. As I've stated, we *choose* to allow outside circumstances dictate our inner frame of mind, both good and bad. Sure, there are annoying people and situations all around us, but how we *react* remains our decision. This is directly proportional to the amount of stress we experience.

There are judgments and decisions that we make on a moment-to-moment basis that we aren't even consciously aware of. William Shakespeare's character Hamlet said, "There is nothing either good or bad, but thinking makes it so." What we judge to be "good" or "bad" is entirely a matter of how we view the world.

I've heard that people tend to have one of two views of the world. One is that the world and the people in it are inherently good. The other is that the world is inherently evil. Glass full. Glass empty. Most of us fall somewhere along the spectrum between the two extremes.

How we view ourselves can change from time to time. Sometimes we're "up" on ourselves. Sometimes, we're not. There is wonderful little exercise that can help keep us in balance:

Keep two truths in your pocket and take them out
according to the need of the moment. Let one be
'For my sake the world was created.'
And the other: 'I am dust and ashes.'

—Rabbi Simcha Bunam Bonhart (1765–1827)

An abbreviated version would be "I rock" and "I suck." Same concept. I think the key is to never have to reach into our pockets for either paper, but rather maintain a healthy, balanced perspective of ourselves.

Confrontation

At this point in my life, I tend to avoid confrontation. My life philosophy can be summed up neatly, "Why crack a sweat? Why break a nail?" I ought to have that embroidered on a set of pillows.

I used to be somewhat argumentative when I was in my twenties and thirties, especially when alcohol was involved. I was also a bit of a contrarian, always playing devil's advocate and taking the opposing position. A little of that went a long way, both for me and the people I was brow-beating with my opposing point of view.

I've learned that life is too short to try to change Other People's views. As Mahatma Ghandi said, "You must be the change you want to see in the world." Far better to live your philosophies and have people drawn to you than to attempt to *force* your beliefs on them. More often than not, it just makes people resistant anyway.

I've come to the realization that people basically believe what suits them. It's difficult to pry people out of their comfort zone if they don't want to be budged. So, what's the point? That might involve cracking a sweat *and* breaking a nail.

Another great saying is, "If you want to change the world, start with changing yourself." And let's not forget this George Carlin adage: "You can pick your friends and you can pick your nose, but you can't pick your friend's nose." Lord knows, I've overstepped my bounds on *that* one too many times to count. Know your limitations.

Fight or Flee?

When someone says something offensive we have choices as to whether or not we are going to:

1. Stay and fight.

2. Walk away and refuse to lend the situation or person our time, energy, and talent.

We often find ourselves at a crossroads where we must choose whether or not to enter a potential battle. Most of the time, we are barely conscious of it, but we are still deciding minute-by-minute whether or not we are going to react to outside irritations. It can be the small stuff, like whether or not to react to a personal affront, such as someone prefacing every remark with, "*at your age*." Or it can be a larger, more insulting remark or action.

Some people thrive on confrontation and seek it out every chance they get. They are addicted to the adrenaline rush produced by the "fight" part of the "fight or flight" mechanism. Other people avoid altercations as much as possible, much preferring to flee. There has to be a balance. Not every dispute is worth fighting. But, unless we have chosen to go through life as a doormat, we will likely find ourselves in a scuffle from time to time. We can still choose how much we are going to let it affect us.

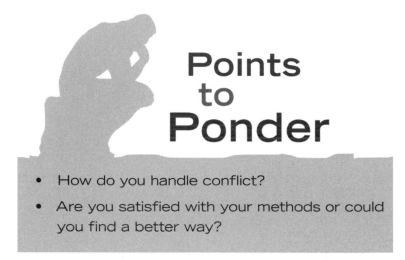

Points to Ponder

- How do you handle conflict?
- Are you satisfied with your methods or could you find a better way?

PART II

A Whole Mess o' Stress

CHAPTER NINE

....

The Distress of Stress

The man who doesn't relax and hoot a few hoots voluntarily now and then is in great danger of hooting hoots and standing on his head for the edification of the pathologist and trained nurse a little later on.

—Elbert Hubbard (1856–1915)

Stress is one of those words that gets bandied about a lot, but just what *is* it? In a nutshell, stress is our body's response either to internal or external circumstances. Pain, for example, would be an internal circumstance. An unannounced visit from the inlaws would be an external circumstance.

Apparently, when we are stressed out by these situations, we secrete a couple of hormones: cortisol and adrenaline. These little chemical message delivery-men put us in "fight or flight" mode. Our hearts begin pounding. Our breathing becomes shallow. Our blood vessels constrict. Our muscles grow tense.

"Fight or flight" was a useful mechanism for our distant ancestor, the caveman when he had his anxious moments. When he encountered a bear on his path, for example, he had to make the split second decision to stay and fight the beast or run away. Nowadays, though, the problem is that we tend to keep ourselves in this constant state of life-or-death readiness even though there is no impending threat of death or doom.

High levels of cortisol and adrenaline pumping through our bodies is useful, say, if you are competing in the World's Strongest Man contest and are bench-pressing a roll top desk. But, when was the last time you actually ran across a bear? Unless you live at the zoo, it's highly unlikely that it was any time recently.

I saw a man who *looked* like a bear, but that was due to his freakish amount of body hair. At least I *think* he was a man. He might have been a werewolf. I'm not really sure since I didn't get a good look at his teeth.

The Stress of Negativity

We tend to judge ourselves and others for so-called negative emotions. But the truth is they are a natural part of the human experience: anger, frustration, and fear. In and of themselves, they aren't "bad." But, we should allow negative emotions to be like messengers. We should take a look at them and see what they are telling us. We should only allow negativity to be a brief visitor and not move in as a full time resident. Nobody likes a whiner.

Laugh, and the world laughs with you;
Weep, and you weep alone.

—Ella Wheeler Wilcox (1855–1919)

My version is:
Laugh, and the world laughs with you;
Weep, and people will cross to the other side
of the street to avoid you. I'm just saying.

—Kay Frances (1955–)

Even our loved ones will only show empathy for our troubles to a point. I'm not talking about legitimate problems, but unfounded chronic negativity will not only drive people away, but will eventually cause our own health to deteriorate. Of course, if there are people you *want* to drive away or you're a fan of poor health, whine more!

I'm not saying that we should be like those eternal optimists. You know these people? Always "on," always happy, happy, happy! Aren't they just annoying to the rest of us when we're trying to enjoy a big, fat, pity party? "Look on the bright side, you could be dead!" You're thinking, "So could you. One could only hope."

We need to maintain a spirit of *realistic* optimism. The key is to monitor our thoughts. It's amazing how often they drift off to the past or the future, many times with an accompanying feeling of regret or foreboding. Have you ever seen someone who can recount a slight or snub that happened years ago as though it was yesterday? They can get themselves in a red-faced frenzy over an event that has long since passed.

Sure, sometimes it's fun to wallow in negativity and we all enjoy recounting a good snub now and then. It can make for a great story and if we're being honest, we all enjoy a good pity party from time to time. Sometimes it's even fun to play, "I've-been-a-bigger-victim-than-you!" or "Let's-see-whose-life-sucks-the-most!" But, when we overdo the wallowing, it begins to wear on our health. It's not that we should totally forget every negative thing that has ever happened to us. Most of the time, it's best to retain the lesson without the attached emotion. Better yet, just let it go.

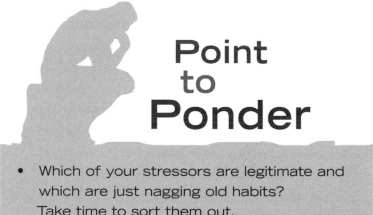

Point to Ponder

- Which of your stressors are legitimate and which are just nagging old habits?
  Take time to sort them out.

Let the Sun Shine In

We don't need to go through life like Teflon, letting everything slide off of us. Nor do we have to build walls around ourselves, never letting anything touch us. I prefer to think of myself as surrounded by cheesecloth. I let things through, but filter the content. Plus, everyone knows if you put cheesecloth over a camera lens, it will make you look younger. So by surrounding yourself with cheesecloth, not only can you better manage your stress, but it's a great anti-aging tactic.

Mama's Advice

A certain amount of fear and worry is to be expected, but the problem is that we waste too much time and energy on *unnecessary* fretting. My mom used to say that 90% of what we worry about never happens. I think this is true. But, this is also the person who told me to wear clean underwear in case I got into an accident. Like that's the best reason she could come up for changing your drawers! If not for caring what those paramedics might think of me, I'd wear the same ol' pair, week in and week out.

Mom's underwear theories were flawed, but I think she was dead on about pointless worrying.

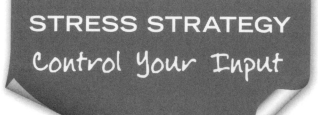

STRESS STRATEGY
Control Your Input

People say, "But Kay, you don't understand! Look at my life! You'd live in a constant state of upset, too!"

I'm not saying we don't have reasons to be distressed. We have plenty to worry about: the economy, terrorism, who's going to win the reality show du jour. We have plenty of reasons to not want to get out of bed in the morning. First of all, the bed is warm and comfortable and the world is not. Seems like a pretty easy choice to me.

Some days it's best not to let the outside world enter our consciousness. We can control much of our input and it's often wise to do so. It's not easy, but it's often the only choice we have. So, lay down those newspapers and step away from the eleven o'clock news occasionally. The world will keep on spinning and you'll be surprised at how much peace of mind you'll have by tuning out all of that negativity.

....

Every moment we spend fretting over the future or lamenting the past is a moment not spent in the only thing within our control: the present. Learn from the past, take good care of today, and you'll create the future you desire.

Points to Ponder

- How much time do you spend thinking about the past or future?
- What can you do to control the input to your mind?

CHAPTER TEN

....

Heaps o' Peeps

*You are the average of the five people
you spend the most time with.*

—Jim Rohn (1930–2009)

Whether you are young, old, single, divorced, widowed, or married, it is still important to have a good network of people in your life. While many of our needs can be met in our primary relationship such as our spouse or significant other, it's still important to have a wide range of people in our lives that fulfill different roles. I really do think we all need a good support system.

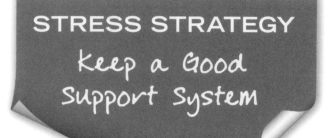

STRESS STRATEGY
Keep a Good
Support System

We need all kinds of people in our network. If we are surrounded by yes men, we'll never grow, but remain stuck in our own inflated opinions of ourselves. If we are surrounded by those who forever wake us up from our fantasies with their well-meaning reality checks, it will wear on us until one day we become lower and smaller than amoebas. That's no kind of life either. Ask any amoeba and it'll tell you, or it would if it had a mouth and opinions.

A good support system requires people who make us laugh and those who let us cry. We need people who support us unconditionally as well as those who give us reality checks from time to time. Problem solvers and good listeners ought to round out our network. I don't feel that all of these characteristics can be found in one person.

Older and Wiser

I think it's important to have friends of all ages. One of my dear friends (and adopted mama) is Barbara, aka "Mama B," who has enjoyed eighty-eight birthday celebrations thus far. She has sisters who are ninety-seven and ninety-eight, so by comparison, she feels pretty young! (It's sort of like how my sister will always feel young in relation to me.)

When a doctor says, "Now Barbara, you're *eighty-eight*!" this does little but perplex her. She asked me one time, "What do they *mean* when they say that? Do they think I'm *old*?" She certainly isn't "old" to me or those that know her.

Mama B has wisdom and a perspective of life that can only come from having been on the planet for awhile. If you don't have older friends, you're missing out on an opportunity to expand and grow. You can't help but learn from people who are farther up the mountain than you are.

Mostly, I hang out with Mama B because she's fun!

The Great Enabler

My sister Carol is in her fortieth year of teaching in the field of special education. I told her that she had already earned her angel wings somewhere around the fifth year of this challenging profession, but she keeps plugging along with no end in sight. Evidently, she not only wants to *go* to heaven but she wants box seats and a reserved parking spot when she gets there.

After forty years on this career path, there is very little my sister hasn't seen or heard. She has had some experiences that would curl your hair. I remember one time a middle school student drew a picture of himself with her. He was wielding a knife and she was bloody from stab wounds. Nice. Not exactly something you want to hang on your refrigerator.

Recently, she was lamenting that a student hadn't shown up for a meeting that day. She went home and turned on the news and saw him, handcuffed, doing the "perp walk" with two police officers. Seems he had robbed a convenience store. He was easy to apprehend because his face was all over the store's surveillance cameras. This whole incident really upset my sister. I said, "Carol, you can't help every kid."

She wailed, "Have I taught these kids NOTHING? If you're going to rob a convenience store, wear a *mask*!"

I would say that a sense of humor has definitely been a must for her in surviving and thriving in her profession. (I could actually cite more heinous examples of what she has endured over the years, but I don't want to impede the relatively light-hearted flow of this book. Plus, I don't want Bloody Knife Kid coming after me.)

Carol is my Great Enabler. No matter what I do, it's fine with her. Because of everything she has seen and been through, it's actually quite hard to shock her. I could go to her and say, "Carol, I robbed a bank."

"Good for you! Please tell me you remembered to wear a mask."

Sometimes we just need to know that we are unconditionally accepted, no matter what. She also has the patience of Job and is extremely easy going. And fun! Did I mention fun? If you don't have a "Carol" in your life, go get one!

The Reality Checker

My younger sister, Cindy, is Ms. Reality Check. She has no problem being blunt or frank but her comments never descend to the level of making me feel like an amoeba (usually just a single-celled organism).

Cindy also maintains moral standards that are higher than most. She's not self-righteous about it, it's just the way she is. If I told her I robbed a bank, she'd grow silent for a moment then say, "Kay, that's wrong and I'm telling." She probably wouldn't in the end because her loyalty would outweigh her personal convictions, but she would be quick to voice her disapproval. She is a wonderful moral compass.

I go to Cindy when I want The Truth, no matter how ugly. She also has the ability to sort through the chaff and get to the wheat of the matter. People like that are hard to come by. Cherish them if you are fortunate enough to have them in your life. But, just know if you rob a bank, you're taking your chances if you confess it to them. Good thing she's fun!

Problem: SOLVED!

My brother, Glenn, is a problem solver. You don't necessarily go to my brother for empathy or sympathy (you might get it, you might not). You approach Glenn if you want an issue solved logically and methodically.

If I told him I got caught trying to rob a bank, he would not want to hear how I *feel* about it. He also has little patience for a foolish act like bank robbery. (There's no figuring some people.) He'd likely respond:

> [Sigh] You didn't know that's against the law? Do you realize the kind of headaches this will generate for law enforcement officials? Thank God for FDIC so the people's deposits are insured. Wait. You didn't rob *my* bank, did you? Did you wear a mask? I don't want any of the tellers knowing my sister did this. Okay, I'll give you the number of a good attorney. Call right away. DON'T use my name. I have to go. Don't call here again. [Sigh] How much money are you going to need for bail? It's going to be mighty embarrassing having to walk into the bank to get it. Kay this is NOT FUNNY!

I might not like what I hear, but I will get the information that I need. My brother would help me, but not without a lecture first. I figure he owes me after all of the whoopings I endured from him when we were kids. If he *doesn't* help me, I can always threaten him my old standby, "You've got to sleep *sometime*!" (I do concede that what is "cute" when said by a little girl is kind of disturbing coming from a middle-aged woman.)

Go get yourself a Glenn. Or you can borrow mine. Since I haven't robbed a bank in awhile, he's not busy getting bail money together or lecturing me about The Law.

Oh yeah, and he's fun, too! Are you seeing a pattern in the people I choose to surround myself with?

Vampires Among Us

Sometimes we find ourselves in totally toxic and lopsided relationships that are virtually devoid of "give and take." Well, not "devoid" so much as one person does all the giving (you) and the other does all the taking (them).

I had a so-called friend who would call and ask me how I was doing. Without waiting for the answer, she would launch into a tirade of her problems and issues du jour. High drama swirled around this woman and she thrived on it.

I finally realized that listening to *her* problems gave me a nice diversion from my own. Watching the events of her life unfold was a little like watching a bad horror movie without the resolution at the end. She would voluntarily keep going back into "the house with the monster" again and again with no end in sight. It was exhausting.

The problem with unbalanced relationships like this is that at some point it becomes like the relationship between a host and a parasite. These people are time and energy vampires who latch on and suck the life force from people leaving a trail of limp, lifeless carcasses behind them. And we all know how painful *that* can be!

When you don't have the time or energy for them, they will turn on you like Dr. Jekyll and become insufferable and demanding. And those are their assets!

These are people who will declare you their "best friend" two months into the association. When this happens, I always wonder how many people they've chewed up and spit out along the way. These people are toxic and best avoided at all costs.

Cut them loose as soon as you realize what you're dealing with. I don't mean to avoid them or continue telling them you're "busy." They will never get the hint. Tell them "buh-bye"! Don't worry about hurting their feelings. They will quickly find new prey. You can't win with these people no matter what you do. So cut your losses and run like a scared rabbit! You know I'm right. You can't possibly want to become a limp, lifeless carcass. I mean really. Given the choice, I'd rather be an amoeba. Maybe it's just me.

....

Good friends make life so much richer. I'm truly thankful for the great people I've had the good fortune to know and the many wonderful folks I can call "friends." I wish the same for you. One thing I've learned over the years is that the best way to *have* a good friend is to *be* a good friend.

Points to Ponder

- Who makes up your support system?

- Are the people in your life fun? Not every minute of every day, but for the most part?

- Do you need to take inventory of the people in your life and make any changes? Are all of your needs being met?

- Do you need to engage in a "friend detox"?

CHAPTER ELEVEN

....

Steer Clear of Fear

Only when we are no longer afraid do we begin to live.

—Dorothy Thompson (1893–1961)

Taking a good look at our fears doesn't necessarily require us to change anything. It merely requires that we get honest with ourselves about what our fears are, and then decide if we are going to endeavor to work through them or accept them and live with them. What should *not* be on our menu of choices is to continue to stress over them.

One working definition of insanity is, "doing the same thing over and over and expecting different results." Going around and around with ourselves is futile, unhealthy, and unproductive.

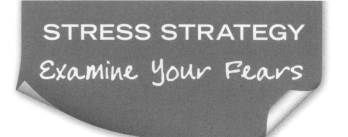

STRESS STRATEGY
Examine your Fears

Fear is one of our biggest stressors. In and of itself it is not a bad thing. It alerts us of impending danger and can be a useful messenger. The problem is when we are gripped by chronic trepidations that prevent us from living our fullest lives. This happened to me, and as a result I had two years of psychotherapy. I was then able to work through some issues that had me frozen in my tracks.

Of all the illogical afflictions to have, I found I had a fear of success. Sounds foolish now, but it was very real at the time and I was (unconsciously) doing everything in my power to sabotage my success. I've since put an end to THAT baloney!

Fear of Failure

An inventor fails 999 times, and if he succeeds once, he's in. He treats his failures simply as practice shots.

—Charles Kettering (1876–1958)

Fear of failure is one of our most prevalent anxieties. This is easily rectified if we realize that:

- If we aren't failing, we aren't trying.

- It's not how many times we fall down; it's how many times we get back up.

- [Insert your own "failure" adage here.]

My sister Cindy would probably say,

- "It's not how many times you fail; it's how many times *your elevator goes to the top.*"

One of my favorite adages is, "Don't give up five minutes before the miracle." How do we know when we are at the point where we could take just one more step to get the desired result or even realize our dreams? How many times do we quit too soon? Let's take a lesson from inventors and view our so-called failures as "practice shots."

"Cuckoo for Cocoa Puffs"

Another common feeling is the worry of being thought "crazy." I blame the movie, *One Flew Over the Cuckoo's Nest* for the irrational terror that many of us have about being deemed certifiably insane and banished to a mental hospital until the end of time.

On some level, we have this pathological dread of being attached to some sort of shock machine against our will and spending the rest of our lives drooling on ourselves and seeing imaginary insects everywhere. This fear runs so deep that it prevents people from getting the help they need. People think nothing of going to the hospital for a bleeding wound, but balk at taking care of the gaping wound in their soul. The stigma attached to mental illness in this country is appalling. Crazy, really.

I suspect many of us think *we* are sane and it's the rest of the world that's crazy. Like the old saying goes, "The whole world is crazy except for me and thee and lately I've been wondering about *thee*." Add it to the list of self delusions we all suffer from: "I can sing, I'm a good driver and it's *everyone else* that's crazy."

By the way, I mean no disrespect to mental health professionals or their patients when I toss around the word, "crazy." After all, I've *been* a patient. But, I believe there is such a thing as being "crazy in a good way."

"Call me crazy!"

If no one ever calls us crazy, we either aren't taking enough chances or we aren't having enough fun.

—Kay Frances (1955–)

We don't want to be called "crazy" every day. But, from time to time, we should have an idea or a plan that makes people look at us as though we have poppy seeds stuck in our teeth.

"You want to do *what*??"

Excessive worry about what Other People think can get a grip on us if we're not careful. This will prevent us from straying too far from "normal." I learned a long time ago that "normal" isn't even a remotely worthy goal.

Sometimes we imagine that everyone is consumed with thoughts and judgments of us. The truth is they are too absorbed in their *own* lives to spend much time giving us much thought one way or another. If they *are* thinking about us, they are wondering what *we* are thinking about *them*.

If you limit your actions in life to things that nobody can possibly find fault with, you will not do much.

—Charles Lutwidge Dodgson
(Lewis Carroll), (1832–1898)

Fear of the Unknown

Many of us suffer from the fear of the unknown particularly when it comes to the future. We worry about financial insecurity, employment instability, and national and global unrest. There are real and legitimate reasons to be concerned, even scared. But, it's just as easy to imagine a future that is secure as it is to imagine one that is full of peril.

The future hasn't happened yet, but we are molding our experiences with our thoughts and actions in the present. It's surprising how much control we really have over our own destinies if we just choose to exercise it. Why not look at the unknown as an adventure?

Fear of Aging

Many people are frightened by the prospect of aging. As the old saying goes, "Getting older is not a bad thing when you consider the alternative." If we're being totally honest, deep down, many of us have the fear of ending up old, alone, broke, and homeless.

Frankly, we're afraid of ending up like this lady. Would that be so bad? I actually think she looks pretty happy! And no one can say she isn't expressing her individuality.

What's the Worst That Can Happen?

A lot of our fears are completely irrational. Oftentimes, we don't even know where they came from or if they even make sense. We feel apprehensive, but we don't voice it aloud, even to ourselves, and these thoughts just swirl around and around in the dark recesses of our minds. It's vitally important to examine them, sort them out, and then decide what, if anything, we are going to do about them.

Sometimes, if we just shine a light on our deepest, darkest fears, they will dissipate and go away. It is often a matter of going to the end of the thought and this requires vigorous self-talk. We need to ask ourselves:

"What's the worst that can happen?"

"And *then* what?"

"Okay, and *then* what?"

"Okay, and *then* what?"

Anytime a frightful thought raises its ugly head, we can go through this self-dialogue until we discover its root. Through this process, we may find that the particular dread no longer has a hold on us.

Arachnids

I'm not saying we have to overcome all of our fears, only that we examine them. For example, I am afraid of spiders and I can live with it. I don't need to go back into therapy to discover the root cause and work through that fear. By the way, the best thing for spiders is hairspray. It doesn't kill them, but their hair looks good for days. They'll eventually leave on their own thinking, "I'm looking way too good for this dump. I'm out of here."

Points to Ponder

- What are you afraid of? I mean really afraid of?
- Are any of these fears preventing you from living the life you want?
- What can you do about them?

CHAPTER TWELVE

···

A Yearning for Learning

Anyone who stops learning is old,
whether at twenty or eighty.

—Henry Ford (1863–1947)

*L*ifelong learning enhances our lives and gives us a much wider range of experiences. It's empowering to learn about and master new things. There is also much evidence to support the assertion that people who continue to learn and exercise their brains have a greater chance of retaining mental acuity in middle age and beyond than those who don't.

STRESS STRATEGY
Always Keep Learning

My mom and dad both spent thirty years of their lives as school teachers, so I'm sure it comes as no surprise that they were huge proponents of education. My siblings and I were raised with the mantra, *"When* you go to college . . ."* not *"If* you go to college . . ." But, beyond formal education, they taught us that what was most important was to be resourceful and always keep learning and expanding our horizons.

MUSING

Being raised by two teachers wasn't the easiest experience in the world. If I came home from school and complained that a teacher didn't like me, my folks didn't go marching into the school, demanding to know why the teacher was picking on their little darling. Their response to "teacher doesn't like me" was, "Well, you better get real likable!"

My dad believed that you could learn most anything from a book. He taught himself to tune and repair pianos from how-to manuals and developed a nice side business which he had for many years.

"Educated Fool"

One summer, Dad developed a fascination with horse racing and decided to buy a horse. He only spent a few hundred dollars on this animal, and got some books to learn how to train it.

The old guys at the county fairgrounds who had been raising and racing horses all of their lives got a huge kick out of watching my dad attempt to turn this "hairy old pasture filly" into a race horse. They called him an "educated fool." This didn't deter my dad. He took all of his time, attention and newly found knowledge and attempted to turn Cut-a-Caper into a contender.

Note: Standard bred racing is done with a sulky [cart] attached to the back of the horse. The driver rides on the cart unlike thoroughbred racing where the jockey rides on the horse's back.

MUSING

I got to ride on the sulky a few times, and let me tell you, it is FUN! The only downside is when the horse sneezes and shakes her head. The wind catches the—um—"stuff," and it sprays all over you. You start feeling like you are in the front row of a Gallagher concert. (Although I think we can all agree that smashed watermelons in your face are more desirable than horse boogers.) One could live a long, happy life having never gone through that.

Dad began to train Cut-a-Caper and over time, she got stronger and faster. She shed all the hair she had when she came from the pasture and became a sleek and beautiful horse.

When the time came to actually enter her in a race, Dad hired a professional driver. Like jockeys, drivers are small people. My dad was a big man; 6'2", 240 pounds. After having to haul my dad around and around the track, the horse got even faster when the smaller driver came on the scene.

The first time Cut-a-Caper raced, she came in fourth place. She raced the rest of the summer at county fairs all over Ohio and placed first in every subsequent race.

Dad ended up selling Cut-a-Caper for a tidy profit. Last we heard, she went on to have a successful racing career in Florida.

....

There is a huge feeling of satisfaction when we learn something new, whether it's self-taught or acquired from someone else. We are never "too old" to be trained to do our own taxes, to be proficient on the computer, or study anything else that captures our interest.

Points to Ponder

- What have you always wanted to do?
- What's preventing you from doing it?
- There's no time like the present and it's never "too late."

....

Karate

A journey of a thousand miles begins with a single kick.

—Kay Frances (1955–)

As a result of being raised by someone like my dad who had the courage to learn new things in the face of ridicule, I decided to start taking karate.

I had always wanted to study martial arts but I was over forty years old when I finally did it. It was on my list of things to do before I died. I figured I'd better get with it because I didn't think Medicare covered injuries sustained from karate.

Of course when you do something that is considered a bit "crazy" or a bit "inappropriate" for your age, there are going to be naysayers. This friend of mine said, "You can't take karate! You're too *old*. You'll never keep up with those young people. *At your age*, you could break a hip!" I thought she could be right, but I didn't think I was too old to learn a little self-defense and get some exercise. It wasn't as though I thought I was going to be the next Jackie Chan; the next big martial arts action star. What movie would I be in?

- *Crouching Tiger, Hidden Arthritis?*

- How about *Curse of the Saggin' Dragon?*

- Or maybe *Spider Vein?*

Three and half years into my studies, much to my amazement and gratitude, I was awarded a black belt in karate. I even got a tattoo to commemorate the occasion. It's just a little tiny Japanese symbol for "karate" on my hip. At least I *think* it says "karate." For all I know it says, "Kick me."

空
手

Karate? Kick me? Who can say?

Learn from Children

Shortly after receiving my black belt, my instructor left our local YMCA and I became the head karate instructor for the next seven years. I was amazed at what I was able to learn from my students, especially the youngsters.

I had a student who I'll call "Austin" who was possibly the smartest person I'd ever known. At the age of eight, he had a photographic memory that was astounding. During his first class, he learned a series of fighting motions that takes most people a month to learn.

But what was so admirable and endearing about Austin was his total lack of humility. When I would compliment him on how smart he was or what a good job he was doing, he'd put his hands on his little hips and matter-of-factly reply, "I *know!*" You just don't *do* that in our society! But, Austin was pure. He had not learned the art of false modesty. I complimented him frequently just to hear him say, "I *know!*"

When did low self-esteem become fashionable anyway? Shouldn't we all be more like Austin? If you want to really disarm someone, next time you're given a compliment, instead of doing the usual "aw shucks" routine, just proudly say, "I *know!*" It's worth it just to see the expression on the person's face.

Children don't hold back. When they want to laugh, they laugh. Kids will even laugh when it's "inappropriate" because they haven't learned to control that response. I suspect they instinctively know that laughter reduces stress, so they giggle sometimes when they are scared or in trouble. They are not even consciously aware that they are just trying to feel better. They are merely exercising a totally normal human instinct. Somewhere along the way, we learn to suppress that.

We all know that we need to lighten up, so why are we so darned serious? Oh yes. Because we are *adults* with *adult responsibilities*. But we can learn from children. Kids don't have near the stress we have. (Of course, they don't have jobs, mortgages, and *kids*.) But if a child doesn't like what you're saying, they don't sit silently and chew and stew over it. They cover their ears and say, "I'm not listening! LA LA LA LA!" Wouldn't it be nice if *we* could do that? Cover our ears in some boring meeting and shout, "I'm not listening! LA LA LA LA!" Hey, why not? What's the worst that can happen? At the least the meeting would instantly get more interesting.

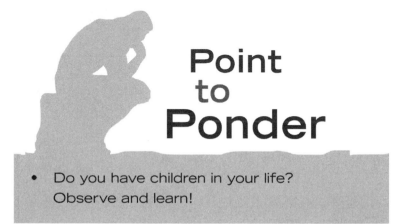

Point to Ponder

- Do you have children in your life? Observe and learn!

....

CHAPTER THIRTEEN

A Wealth of Good Health

The human body is the best picture of the human soul.

—Ludwig Wittgenstein (1889–1951)

When you come from a place of inner peace, optimal health, and balance, you are better equipped to manage external and internal stress factors. Plus, you can leap off tall buildings with a single bound which is soooo much quicker than taking the elevator.

STRESS STRATEGY
Maintain Good Health

Health Nut

I admit it. I've become one of those people I used to hate: a health nut. But, please understand that I'm not preaching from an ivory tower here. As I touched on earlier, I have done about everything I could have possibly done to ruin my health. In college and well beyond, I never met a drink or drug I didn't like. I started smoking cigarettes at the age of seventeen and puffed my way into my forties before quitting.

My dietary habits over the years have been hit-and-miss. I had never had a weight problem per se, but that's probably because I couldn't wait to stop eating so I could get to my after-meal smoke. But that all changed when I quit smoking. I replaced my nicotine habit with an addiction to sugar and carbohydrates and swiftly put on forty pounds.

So, when it comes to bodily self-abuse, I'm not judging anyone! I'm just saying that there came a point when the unhealthy methods I used to manage my stress just didn't work anymore. In fact, they created more problems than they helped to solve. Unhealthy coping mechanisms are only effective in the short run.

"Generics"

The primary impetus for turning my health around was when I reached the age of forty and took a good look at the genetic hand I had been dealt. None of my grandparents made it to age sixty. If it's all just about "family history," I have about five minutes left to live. Seriously, I'm feeling a little faint. I don't even think I'm going to make it through this chapter.

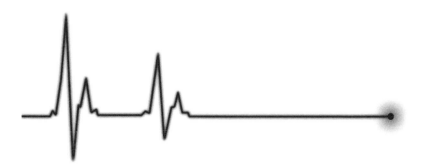

(Okay, I'm back. Apparently, a paramedic came by and resuscitated me. Thank God I was wearing clean underwear.) With my family history and never knowing how close I am to death, I have to wear good undergarments *all the time*. It's exhausting!

Luckily for people like me, it isn't all about genetics. It is estimated that the state of our health is about 25–30% genetics and 70–75% lifestyle choices. This means we have a lot of control over our well-being.

MUSING

I told my doctor, "I'm worried, especially about the heart disease and cancer in my family."
He said, "Oh, don't worry about cancer."
Brightening, I said, "Oh, really?"
"Really. Because heart disease is going to get you loooong before cancer ever will!"
Thanks, Doc. I feel better already.

MUSING

Quote from an actual drug ad: "For the medication to work properly, it must be taken as prescribed. It will not work if you stop taking it." I have to take it? Here I thought I just had to sit and think about taking it!

Mama's Advice

I do believe that nothing will zap the mind, body, and spirit like poor physical health. The worse condition our bodies are in, the more ill-equipped we are to deal with the challenges we face.

I've further come to believe that good health is based on the "little" things our moms told us:

- "Go outside and play!"

- "Drink more water."

- "Eat your fruits and vegetables."

- "Get plenty of sleep."

- "Don't run with scissors."

And let's not forget the whole underwear thing.

Look to your health; and if you have it, praise God, and value it next to a good conscience; for health is the second blessing that we mortals are capable of; a blessing that money cannot buy.

—Izaak Walton (1593–1683)

Exercise

I don't want to beat a dead horse here (has anyone ever actually DONE that? What an awful expression), but it's vitally important that we make time for exercise. Park far away. (For one thing, parking away from all of the Other People will lessen your chances of getting door dings on your car.) Take the stairs. Walk. And remember: "lack of time" is no excuse! We all have twenty-four hours a day. If we don't find time for wellness, we'll have to find time for sickness.

....

I am endeavoring to live a long and healthy life. But I don't necessarily want to live to be one-hundred, nor do I think it's probable; partly because of the "30% genetics" factor and also due to the earlier abuses I imposed upon my body. This doesn't stop me from doing what I can to maintain a strong and healthy body.

At this point, I basically, I have three goals in life:

1. Refuse to focus on or accept my family history.

2. Feel good while I'm here.

3. Outlive my sister so I won't be buried with that pink dryer sheet.

If I do live to be one-hundred, I want to be this lady.

Oh yeah! I'm smoking! And drinking! At one-hundred I'll do what I want. I'm even having nude pictures taken and putting them all over the Internet.

....

When it comes to health, the physical, mental, emotional, and spiritual parts of us are all tied together. If one area is out of balance, the others will surely follow.

Points to Ponder

- Are you satisfied with your health?
- What do you need to do to have the level of health you desire?
- When will you start doing it?

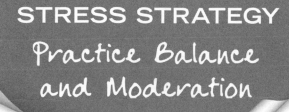

STRESS STRATEGY

Practice Balance and Moderation

Cheating with Cheetos

Even though one of my primary life goals is to thumb my nose at my family history and live a long, healthy life I still believe that we have to *live*. To me, it's all about balance and moderation. We can enjoy those little treats that life has to offer as long as it's infrequent and not overdone.

Even being a health and wellness advocate, I admit that I can "get my Cheeto on." I can eat some Cheetos! And they're about the worst thing you can eat. Have you ever read the bag? They've got substances not known to nature. But I love them! I love that fake cheese. I love that crunch. And if you eat enough of them, you get that big, edible fake cheese glove on your hand. Then you lick one finger at a time. That is *good eatin'*! But, they defy the laws of physics. You can eat a one-pound bag of Cheetos and gain three pounds. How can this be? Do they just keep puffing up in your stomach?

Some foods are triggers for me and I know that I have to avoid them. I define "trigger foods" as follows: when one turns to twenty. In other words, you *plan* to eat "just one" but before you know it, you've eaten *twenty*. The most glaring example of one of my trigger foods is miniature candy bars—the "fun" size. I used to justify that I was burning off the calories with all that unwrapping. Oh, I was feeling the burn! The lies we tell ourselves. [Sigh]

I also have a tendency to overeat when I'm stressed. I have amassed quite a few healthy coping mechanisms over the years, but from time to time, a big fat bowl of ice cream is the only antidote.

Some people *can't* eat when they're stressed. The rest of us hate them. These are the people who will lament, "I was so upset last year that I couldn't even eat! Why twenty pounds just *fell off of me!*" (I don't know about you, but pounds simply "falling off" is an entirely foreign concept to me.)

These are the same people that will take one bite of cheesecake then push it away claiming, "It's too *rich*!"

Those words have never left my lips.

Worse are the people who go to an all-you-can-eat dessert bar and get all excited. Not over the chocolate fountain. Instead, they gush, "Oh look! They've got *fruit*!" I'm sorry, but fruit is not dessert; it's medicine.

I'll be the first to admit that given the choice between chocolate cake and an apple, I'd take the cake every time. But, I usually don't because I realize there are consequences attached to that choice. Every now and then, yes; every day, no. It really comes down to monitoring our choices and being willing to accept the consequences of them.

MUSING

If you "are what you eat," I'm an egg white.
I've never felt so attractive.

I do feel much better when I maintain a diet rich in fruits and vegetables with adequate protein and fiber. And water—lots and lots of water. Our bodies are over 70% water and we need fluid, especially water.

Despite the many diet crazes and fads, it's my opinion that they haven't been able to improve upon the food pyramid and the five basic food groups (they changed it from four). It really is that simple. We make life so much harder than it needs to be.

Alcohol

There is nothing inherently wrong with drinking alcohol as a means of relieving tension. As a matter of fact, it's widely undisputed that drinking red wine in moderation is very good for staving off heart disease and can be an asset to one's health. But, since the word "moderation" was missing from my personal dictionary, I had to give up drinking altogether. See, by *my* way of thinking, if a *glass* is good, then a fifty-five gallon *drum* is even better!

One of the worst memories of my drinking days was the time I overdid it on peppermint schnapps. I was puking candy canes and it was *not* pretty.

"Is this my stop?
How about *this* one?"

For you folks who like to enjoy a few cocktails now and then, I say, "Go for it!" I don't have a particular moral objection to drinking or anything else that adults choose to do with their bodies. I do stand by my philosophy: "Everything in balance and moderation." I still believe that adults should be free to make the choices that work for them. However, I learned long ago, that even one drink was not going to work for me.

There was a specific point when I knew it was time to give up alcohol. There's something about being falling-down drunk and lost on a subway by yourself in New York City at 2:00 a.m. that will make you rethink your use of the sauce. If I had a guardian angel, I figured he or she was getting mighty tired of rescuing me from myself; it was time to do my part.

I also have a tongue-in-cheek theory that we are dealt a certain number of "good luck" cards at birth. I had so many alcohol related close calls over the years that I figured I couldn't possibly have many cards left.

And since I was living in a place like New York City, I felt I needed all of my faculties. I also sensed that it wouldn't be prudent to be going down to Times Square to score weed. I guess you could say I was scared straight. So, nineteen years ago, I gave up alcohol and drugs, one day at a time.

Zzzzz's

Getting adequate sleep is one of the best ways of preparing ourselves to handle our day to day anxieties, but we don't get enough of it in this country. It's become almost hip to brag about how little sleep we need to get by:

"I only got four hours of sleep last night."

"Really? I can trump that. I got three hours and forty-five minutes. I win!"

There are many studies that conclude that a lack of sleep can contribute to obesity, diabetes, and a host of other ailments. Let's all get more shut-eye and make it hip to be a rack hound. Boast that you got eight hours of sleep and are proud of it!

....

Endeavor to "live" and enjoy the things in life you want to indulge in, bearing in mind the importance of keeping everything in balance and in moderation.

MUSING

You know you're getting older when fiber intake and bowel movements become fascinating topics of conversation.

SOME SIMPLE
STRESS BUSTERS

Make lists • LAUGH • Take a deep breath
Exercise • Take naps • Sing a song • Eat right
Ask others for help • Call a friend • Ride a bike
Prioritize tasks • Delegate work • Avoid clutter
Have a hobby • BREATHE • Plant a garden
Shop! • Learn to say "no" • Avoid junk food
Drink WATER • Get organized • Screen calls
Reframe problems as challenges
Read good books • Cry sometimes
Make whoopee! • Have the occasional pity party
Enjoy the small things • Stretch • Listen to music
Scream in a pillow • Hug it out • RELAX
Take it one day at a time • Don't procrastinate
Go to the movies • Have good friends
Keep a journal • Volunteer • Go camping
Take a walk • Spend time in nature • Pet an animal
Pet a human (get permission first!)
Watch your weight • Vacation
Take a class • Prepare • Dance
Keep a clear conscience • Plan ahead
Get enough sleep • Get plenty of "me" time
Meditate • Sleep late • Eat good chocolate
Get a pedicure • Seek counseling

I asked a lady in a stress management workshop I was giving what she did to relieve stress. Staring straight ahead with a cold, distant look in her eye she replied, "Hire a hit man." That might just relieve the stress of all involved. I'm just saying.

Point to Ponder

- What other stress busters do you employ in your life?

CHAPTER FOURTEEN

··

The Funny Thing About Longevity

*One great thing about getting old is that you can get
out of all kinds of social obligations
simply by saying you're too tired.*

—George Carlin (1937–2008)

I have come to believe that there are many factors for
living a long and healthy life. I've learned this from
observing those who have done it. I've also reviewed
the evidence that supports the notion that managing
our stress, taking care of our health, and keeping a
positive attitude are among the common denominators
for those that not only reach old age, but enjoy it.

Pearl

I had a neighbor named Pearl who lived to be 103. She lived alone in her own home until she was 101. You would see Pearl out in her yard, tending to her flowers and mowing her lawn with a *manual* push mower (not a gas powered mower).

Pearl was a very funny, upbeat, and positive person. It was fun to go visit her and when you did so, you had to call and make an appointment because Pearl was very busy. She had many friends and an active social life.

The last time I saw Pearl, she was 101 and Mom and I went to visit her. Pearl helped us take *our* coats off, and then we sat and enjoyed a nice visit.

Mom and Pearl had been teachers at the same school years before that and had carpooled together. Pearl always had great stories of those times. That day, Pearl said, "Eleanor [my mom], do you remember the time we were going to school and I was driving, Mary Lou Berger was in the passenger seat and you were in the back seat?"

Mom replied, "Well, which time are you talking about, Pearl? We rode together for years."

"Well, on this particular morning, we drove past this house and there was a *naked man* standing in the picture window. Do you remember it *now*, Eleanor?"

Mom had a great sense of humor but she was a little old-fashioned and she was blushing. I said, "Mom! You never told me about this. Well, what happened then, Pearl?"

"Well, your mother missed it, so we had to *drive back by!*"

And she threw her head back and just *cackled!* It occurred to me right there and then that this woman's rich sense of humor, her hobbies, and her active social life are why we were sitting there, enjoying her company at 101 years old.

Pearl died at 103 and her funeral was sad! Normally when someone of this age dies, you figure, "Well, they lived a long life and we all have to go sometime." But people were upset because they were going to *miss* her! I think the only people that weren't upset were the folks at the State Teachers Retirement System. They were probably dancing a jig! "It's about time you got off the system, lady!"

....

Wouldn't it be nice to be a "cool older lady"? Or a "hip older dude"? To be the type of person in their golden years that people *want* to spend time with, not because it makes them feel good about themselves, but because they truly enjoy it!

Some people believe that when your time is up, it's up. In other words, your death date is pre-determined and there is nothing you can do about it. I can't honestly say that I know one way or the other. But even if it's true, I still contend that we have a lot of control over the quality of the time we spend between our birth and our death.

Points
to
Ponder

- How do you want people to think of you in your golden years?

- If you have a choice, would you like to live a long, steady, healthy life? Or would you rather live on the edge, refuse to deny yourself of indulgences, and be a short candle that burns bright? What if it is up to us?

CHAPTER FIFTEEN

....

An Attitude of Gratitude

He is a wise man who does not grieve for the things which he has not, but rejoices for those which he has.

—Epictetus (AD 55–AD 135)

Sometimes, when I'd get too puffed up with my own self-importance, my mom would tell me, "Don't be so full of yourself." I suppose that we need to be knocked down a peg or two from time to time, but overall I think we need to be *more* full of ourselves.

We tend to focus on our shortcomings and don't give ourselves credit for the things we're doing *right*. I think we should celebrate our victories, large and small, and not take them for granted. Be grateful for those seemingly "small" accomplishments.

STRESS STRATEGY
Celebrate Your Victories

I've been off of cigarettes for over thirteen and a half years. Every year I take the money I've saved from quitting and go somewhere special or buy myself something pretty. I was a pack-and-a-half a day smoker and at $4.00/pack, that's $6.00/day, which is $2,190.00/year; $2,196.00 on leap years. I like to think of the savings as a symbol of my victory.

I never want to take that accomplishment for granted. I always want to give myself lots of positive reinforcement for the hardest thing I've ever done. Like most addictions, smoking is insidious and can sneak up and bite you in the backside when you least expect it. Each day, I renew my commitment to good health. I don't think of what I gave up, but what I've gained.

I have had very good blood pressure since I quit smoking. Every time I'm in a store with a blood pressure machine, I take the time to get a reading. It gives me another positive reinforcement and reason to be grateful.

MUSING

If my blood pressure is up a bit that day, I sit and think calm, happy thoughts and keep retaking it until I'm happy with the results. Hey, whatever works! Sometimes, I'm there for hours. I then try to maintain the serenity after I leave the machine. This usually lasts until I get to the U-Scan machine and "she" starts roughing me up.

Great Bones!

I started strength training nearly nine years ago to offset those thinning bones that are an effect of being in menopause. That's right, I'm pumping iron. But, *at my age*, I'm not getting a lot of feedback about it. I don't walk down the street, causing construction sites to come to a complete halt:

"Hey, Joe! Check out the bone density on *that* babe!"

"Woohooo! That's what *I'm* talkin' about!"

So, I brag about my bone density every chance I get.

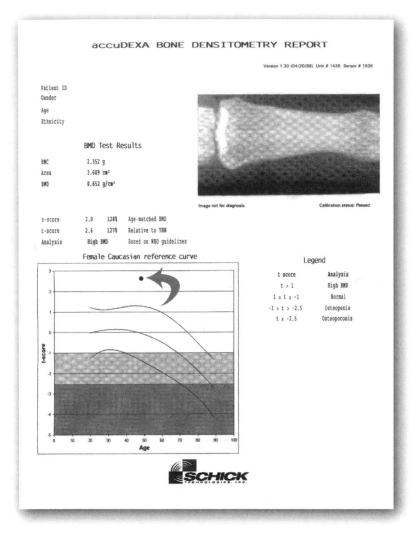

Check out the dot. I'm off the charts! I KNOW! I've stopped people on the street to show them this! I was so proud of this bone density scan that one year I included it with my Christmas cards. I admit I didn't have a lot going on that year. But hey, a lot of my friends send pictures of their kids and grandkids and I don't have any kids (well, none that I *know* of).

Points to Ponder

- What areas of your life are you happiest with?

- Do you take the time to express gratitude and celebrate, even brag a little?

PART III

The Funny Thing About Humor:
The "Big" Stuff

CHAPTER SIXTEEN

....

Laughter: The Best Pill for When You're ILL

Through humor, you can soften some of the worst blows that life delivers. And once you find laughter, no matter how painful your situation might be, you can survive it.

—Dill Cosby (193/–)

*I*t's easy to laugh off small stressors in our day-to-day lives, but can we utilize humor in the more serious matters of life and death? Is it necessary or even appropriate? I contend that humor is required during these difficult times more than ever—when the principles I've outlined thus far are really put to the test.

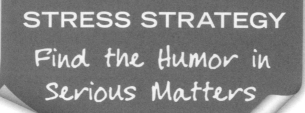

STRESS STRATEGY
Find the Humor in Serious Matters

It was Dad's passing that brought me back to Ohio from New York City where I was in the throes of my career in stand-up comedy. I only intended to stay with Mom for a few months where I felt I was needed and where I wanted to be. But Mom's health was not good. I decided to stay and help her for awhile. One month at a time, a "few months" turned into a seven-year care giving stint.

There were many difficult times and I won't recount all of her afflictions here. As she used to say, "Nobody wants to hear an organ recital."

It was during those years that I quit smoking, started exercising, and began the study of karate. At some level, I knew that I was going to require all of my energy for this important undertaking. I needed good health as well as the emotional and physical boost that exercise provides. And more than ever, I had to find healthy ways to manage my stress. I had already begun my recovery process by giving up alcohol and drugs, but it was time to ramp it up and take it to the next level.

Mom has been gone for eight years and I don't want to whitewash our years together because there were some extremely difficult times. It really doesn't get more serious than terminal illness. But, I will say that humor is one of the tools that helped us both through it.

We found something to chuckle about nearly every day. I saw firsthand what a healing effect laughter had on Mom. It also helped me to maintain my balance and sanity for the largest challenge of my life: caring for the person I had known longer and loved more than anyone else in the world.

Scrabble: An Eight-Letter Word for "No mercy!"

One thing we did to pass the time was to play Scrabble—a LOT of Scrabble. We were extremely competitive and winning was almost a form of blood lust. You would never know we were mother and daughter. But, we had a lot of fun and a ton of running jokes. "The Q can be your friend!"

Sometimes our jokes would get sillier and sillier. When one of us was behind but starting to catch up, we would say, "I'm catching up with you. Can you feel my *sweet breath* on your neck?"

The other would reply in a deep, menacing voice, "Yeah, I feel your breath on my neck. I feel your *hot, putrid, vile* breath on my neck."

It was almost as if we had a script.

Then it became a contest to see how many adjectives we could add. Sometimes our exchanges didn't even make sense. One time Mom said, "I feel your hot, putrid, vile, halitosis, acidosis, *expialidocious* breath on my neck."

Expialidocious breath? Huh? We just roared. I mean we seriously cracked ourselves up. And it felt darned good.

Mom's Daughter, the Blockhead

One year, I dropped Mom off at H&R Block to get her taxes done. I figured it would take about an hour and told her to call me when she was ready to be picked up.

About an hour later, the phone rang. I picked up the phone and growled, "I feel your hot, putrid, vile, halitosis, acidosis, *expialidocious* breath on my phone."

There was a small pause and the man said, "This is H&R Block. Your mother is ready to be picked up."

He wasn't laughing.

I'm surprised he let her get into the car with me! I was just waiting for the call from elder services: "We have a report of you calling a sweet elderly woman '*expialidocious breath*,' care to explain?"

And *she* made it up!

"It's time for the Daily Double!"

Mom and I watched *Jeopardy* almost every night and she was much better at the game than I was. If I didn't know the answer, my standard reply was "Columbus, Ohio." It wasn't unusual for me to shout out this answer twenty or thirty times in a single episode. (Did I mention I'm terrible at *Jeopardy*?)

Imagine my glee when the day finally came when the answer really *was* "Columbus, Ohio." I nearly fainted and Mom had to endure my gloating over that one for weeks. But, she always had to rub it in that I failed to put it in the form of a question.

Picky, picky.

Smiley Mighty Jesus

Mom had a whole team of doctors; one for every body part. I'm not kidding. She even had a dentist *and* a "gum guy."

We got to know some of the doctors pretty well and knowing that Mom and I enjoyed a good laugh, they would share stories. One doctor related the story of a time this lady came in and told him, "Doc, you got to help me. I got the smiley mighty Jesus!"

He said, "The WHAT?"

"The smiley mighty Jesus!"

Turns out she thought she had *spinal meningitis*. Spinal meningitis/smiley mighty Jesus. We've all made that mistake. Turns out it was just gas.

Another patient told the doctor he was pretty sure he had *Cadillacs* in his eyes. Mom and I enjoyed a good laugh over that one. We could only imagine how painful that had to be, especially if it was an older model and the warranty was up; "I'm sorry, sir, we're going to have to operate. If you'd have had Volkswagen Beetles in your eyes, we could've let it slide."

Shake Your Booty!

As you're probably seeing, Mom had a great sense of humor and it was fun to make her laugh. Sometimes I would go to great lengths to do so.

We were coming back from one of her hospital stays in Dayton, Ohio, and we stopped at the grocery store. I needed to run in and pick up a few things and Mom waited in the car. Since we were out-of-town where we didn't know anyone, I got the courage to be really silly. As I was walking away from the car, I stopped and started doing a really silly exaggerated form of dance, shaking my "booty," waving my arms. I looked back and sure enough Mom was laughing, actually a little more than the situation warranted. It wasn't *that* funny.

As I turned around, I almost ran right into Mom's physical therapist from the hospital we had just left. He wasn't laughing. He was giving me that strange half-smile and wide eyes people give you when you've just told them something like, "Silence! I'm receiving information from the home planet!" And he left a really wide distance as he passed me like you would a mad, rabid dog.

Mom, of course, found all of this to be hysterically funny. I tried to explain myself to the guy, "No, see Mom is in the car and I was trying to make her laugh." We looked over at Mom and she shrugged and raised her eyebrows as if to deny being related to me. Or as if to say, "I know she's weird, but she's my *ride*!"

Thanks for having my back, Mom.

The Answer is "No."

At one point, Mom spent over two months in the hospital. She endured more tests, shots, x-rays, transfusions, and chemo than most people do in a lifetime. She joked that with all of that poking and prodding, she should've at least had a tattoo to show for it.

Mom prided herself in being a good patient and went along with everything that was asked of her.

Almost.

My mother wasn't a big fan of answering questions and grew bored quickly. For reasons too complicated to explain here, even though her hospital stay was two months straight, she was moved seven times. Each time they moved her she had to "check in" to the hospital again. Somebody would come around with a clipboard and they would go through the same tired myriad of questions she had already answered the last time they "checked her in."

Mom had little patience for this. I had to listen carefully to both the questions and her answers, ready to run interference. I could see her eyes glaze over and, regardless of the question, all of her answers were "no."

It went something like this:

"Do you have diabetes?"

"No."

"Mom!"

"Oh! Um, yes."

"Do you have any breathing problems?"

"No."

"Mom, you're on oxygen."

"Oh! Yes, I guess I do."

"Are you alive?"

"No."

[Sigh]

"Are you a woman?"

"No."

"MOM!"

"What was the question?"

And on and on.

• •

Though Mom's been gone for eight years, I still miss her terribly. They say you don't "get over" the loss of a loved one, but you do learn to live with it.

To honor her memory, I try to laugh at least once a day. I also make a point to blurt out "Columbus, Ohio!"

for no particular reason from time to time. It probably makes people wonder if I have some kind of State Capital Tourette's Syndrome.

Mom would've wanted it that way.

CHAPTER SEVENTEEN

....

Good Grief

Laughter is a remedy
For sorrow and for care;
It brings joy to troubled souls,
To damaged hearts, repair.

—Sper

Some people may find the title of this section to be off-putting. What can possibly be "good" about grief? It is not my intention to make light of one of the most serious and painful matters of life: the loss of a loved one. I just believe that humor needs to be in the mix.

There are many stages of grief and they are all important, but it is my opinion that humor should be part of the "grief toolbox." I think that laughter is an often overlooked coping mechanism that is vital for surviving this most difficult time of a person's life. Sometimes the laughter comes later, even months after the loss. But whenever it does show, consider it a gift and embrace it whole-heartedly.

Words of Comfort

People always wonder what to say when comforting the bereaved. It means so much when people take the time to send a card or come to the viewing. Not really much has to be said. "I'm so sorry for your loss" covers about any situation. Here are a couple of common comfort phrases that I found odd or humorous in retrospect:

"Your dad is ALWAYS WATCHING."

I didn't want him *always watching* when he was *here*! It's eerie to think that Dad is paying attention to my every little move. I'd really rather he weren't *always* watching. This didn't comfort me as much as frighten me.

"If you need anything—*anything* at all. . . . "

You really can't go wrong with this expression of sympathy and I believe that people really mean it when they say it—to a point. I suppose it could be a problem if the bereaved took it too literally. "Well [sniff] since you offered [sniff], I've been wanting to get that garage built back behind the house for a long time. I know you're pretty handy. . . ."

You get the picture.

"Your mom is in a *better place.*"

All I could think was, "What's wrong with THIS place? How good could it be for Mom if I'm not there?"

I know it's selfish, but I wanted to think she was looking around heaven saying, "The gold streets are quite lovely, but without Kay, it's booooring!"

Mom had such a kind heart. She probably took one look at those pearly gates and wondered how many oysters gave their lives.

Food, Food, and More Food

I think I can safely speak for grieving people everywhere when I say that whatever food items you bring to the bereaved is deeply appreciated. I especially appreciated cakes, cookies, pies, and anything involving chocolate, but that's just my personal preference. It's all good.

I will say this: we got hams, and a lot of them. I don't know what it is about grief that makes people think you crave pork, but if one more ham would've come through that door, I swear I was going to oink! They were still appreciated, nonetheless—all twelve of them. Oink.

Belated Bereavement Humor

My dad had a heart attack and passed away quietly in his sleep. He got an early morning phone call and my mom went to get him. She knew right away that he was gone. She later reported that she felt his forehead and, "it was cool."

Mom always went straight for the forehead. I think she could've hung a shingle as a Psychic Forehead-Feeler. She was amazing. She could "read" what was wrong with you just by this magic forehead touch. No matter what you claimed your ailment was, she'd go right to the forehead. As a kid I can remember that she could tell with one simple pass if you were really sick or just faking it, trying to get out of that test at school. So Mom didn't need a coroner to tell her that her husband of nearly fifty years was gone.

I'm sure it would come as no surprise that my mom found no humor in the fact that her mate had died. However, a few weeks later I got to talking to her about the day Dad died:

I said, "You say he got a phone call?"

She said, "Yes, and I went in to get him. That's when I found out he was gone."

"What did you tell the people on the phone?"

"I told them, 'He can't come to the phone right now. Can I take a message?'"

And then my ultra responsible mom *took a message*! Well, as soon as she said it, she realized how ridiculous this sounded and she and I immediately started laughing. And we laughed and laughed and laughed. I managed to choke out, "Did you tell them that he'd get back to them, but it would have to be *long distance*?" We howled at that one. It was so good to experience the release that laughter provides and to see Mom chuckle once again.

Dad died eight months shy of their fiftieth wedding anniversary. We joked that he was just trying to get out having to get Mom a gift.

My First Big Loss

Dad's death was my first "big loss." I had known and cared about people who had died, but this was the first Big One. I don't have to explain to anyone who has been through this how news like this cuts you to the core; it brought me to my knees.

The next few days after getting the terrible news are still a blur. I was in a mild state of shock and was just told when to be ready, what to wear, and was shuffled from place to place. Here I was a professional stand-up comedian and I could find nothing to smile or laugh about throughout this process, nor would it have been particularly appropriate at that stage.

I remember little bits and pieces of the funeral. The family was left alone with Dad after the memorial service and prior to the burial to say our last goodbyes.

We had all brought items to put in the casket to send along with Dad. I brought a New York City subway map and a token. Don't ask me why I thought that Dad would now want to go to there, seeing how he never wanted to go during his life. And if his disembodied spirit were able to visit the Big Apple, would he really need a map or tokens? I'm sure not claiming that people have rational thoughts during this process but it all made sense at the time. The rituals that I had always thought were a bit strange turned out to be immensely comforting.

My brother brought some loose change. Dad had always said, "If a man has love in his heart and some change in his pocket, he's a rich man." Or maybe my brother thought there were vending machines in heaven. I guess it wouldn't be heaven without them. I can't imagine going through all of eternity without the occasional sweet or salty snack.

People have different ideas about what heaven looks like. I think people project their own ideas onto the concept. I mean, if you get to imagine where or how you'd want to spend all of eternity, wouldn't you want it to reflect all of your personal preferences?

A friend of mine says that in heaven, everyone is thirty years old. I think back on when I was thirty and have no desire to go back there. That would pretty much be hell for me. At thirty, I thought I had everything figured out, but I knew nothing. Plus, I had periods of extreme instability around that time. I suppose I looked better physically, but in some ways, I looked like I wasn't quite "done." Like I needed to go back into the oven for awhile.

MUSING

By the way, wouldn't Cat Heaven sort of be hell for mice? I mean really.

Healing Humor

The evening of Dad's funeral, all of the distant relatives had left, the casserole dishes had been cleared, the hams had been put away, and the only people left were me, my brother, and my two sisters. Mom had already gone to bed and my siblings and I were sitting at the dining room table.

The events of the past few days had left us physically and emotionally exhausted. Yet, we wondered if we were going to be able to sleep that night. After the conversation subsided, we were sitting there, pensive and lost in our own thoughts when all of a sudden, my brother breaks wind. Loudly. My sisters and I just glared at him. I mean really. Of all days. He got this real sheepish look on his face and blurted, "Dad would've wanted it that way!"

We broke into laughter and we laughed and cackled and guffawed. This howl fest went on for at least thirty minutes.

I can't describe the relief, the good feeling that followed that emotional release. In that moment, I knew that I was going to be able to sleep that night, that everything was going to be alright and that I would get through this. Laughter truly is an affirmation of life.

I consider humor to be one of life's greatest gifts. This present isn't offered much in situations like this, but when it is, we have to take it and run with it. During these trying times is when humor will become more than a pleasant feeling, but rather a saving grace. It's easy to apply the principles of humor when times are good, but they are put to the true test in the most serious matters of life and death. When we think it's least "appropriate" is when we need it the most.

Others' Stories

Ever since I've been telling these stories in my presentations, people have been coming up to me and conspiratorially telling me about incidences of humor in their own grief process. I wonder, "Why do we only speak of this in whispers? Why aren't we more accepting of humor's place in these matters?" I contend that it's not only desirable, but vital.

And do people have good stories!

A woman approached me after a presentation and told me that her elderly father had died recently. She then related the story of the day they went to scatter his ashes at sea. There were in Florida and decided that her dad's favorite fishing dock would make an ideal final resting place.

Her mother stood on the end of the pier, poised to empty the urn. They all said a prayer and her mother said to her deceased husband in the container, "I want you to spend all of eternity in the place you loved the best." She emptied the urn, the wind caught the ashes and planted them right squarely back on the woman's crotch. You can imagine the peals of laughter over that one. Maybe his beloved fishing dock was his *second*-favorite place.

Ashes to Ashes

My sister Cindy is the executor of my will and in charge of my final wishes. I have left instructions to be cremated and my ashes scattered over one of my favorite places in the world: an ancient Indian burial effigy in Southern Ohio called Serpent Mound.

Every couple of years, Cindy brings it up: "Now what if I go to scatter them and it's a windy day and you end up all over me?" Lord, hasn't she ever heard of taking a shower? It's going to be a non-issue as I endeavor to outlive her and spare myself the indignity of being cremated and scattered along with that pink dryer sheet. She doesn't know it now, but that thing is going with *her* for all of eternity. However, if I *do* go first, maybe I'll request that she wear a dress made of pink dryer sheets to do the scattering. That'll fix her. I don't know which would upset her more: the pink dryer sheets or being asked to wear a dress.

Actually, she has good reason for concern regarding the ashes ritual. The "scattering of the ashes" always sounds so good in theory, but almost never works as planned.

A friend of mine used to fly for a charter plane company in Arizona. He piloted many trips for people who wanted to scatter a loved one's ashes over the Grand Canyon. Despite his warnings to "lean out!" invariably, they wouldn't and Aunt Millie would end up all over their face. Nobody loves *anybody* enough to want to endure that kind of misfire.

I heard of a family that took their mother's ashes and had coffee mugs made from them. Ick. Sorry, but I think one person's "comfort" is another person's "creepy."

Obituaries

They tell you every detail about a person except *how* the person died! You have to dig through for clues. You check out what organization the donations are requested for in hopes that they'll offer a hint.

I hope I die of something "normal" and standard. I feel badly for people who die in unconventional ways. Take for example the people who are allergic to nuts. Some people have such a serious reaction, they can actually die. That would make for a terrible obituary: "He was killed by some nut."

I'm just saying.

Points to Ponder

- Is there a serious situation in your life that could use more humor?
- What would you want said about you at your memorial service?
- Go to the end of your life and imagine what you would want it to look like as you review the years you spent in this body. Did you leave behind any regrets or "should haves"?

Last Words

If I could choose, I would want to die like Rose, the one-hundred-year-old survivor from the movie *Titantic*. I remember when her love, Jack, was in the icy water, hanging onto the raft that held young Rose. Through chattering teeth, he tells her she *must survive*. Jack assures Rose that her fate is to "die an old lady, warm in your bed." Even if I don't make it to one-hundred, that's how I want to go.

I want to live with the grace, dignity, humor, and curiosity of my mom and dad. I'd like to be courageously sassy and full of myself like my karate student Austin. And someday, I'd like to be a cool older lady like Mama B and Pearl.

Then, when the time comes, I want to die an old lady, warm in my bed just like Rose. Sans pink dryer sheet.

I mean really.

•••••••••••••••••••••••••••••••••••••••

At my memorial service, I'd like them to say the following:

> *If I am not for myself, who will be?*
> *If I am only for myself, who am I?*
> *If not now, when?*
>
> —The Talmud

It's how I've endeavored to live and what I'd like my loved ones to be reminded of for use in their own lives. But for now I think I'll just concentrate on living. Seriously.

AFTERWORD

As within, so without.

—Hermesianax (300 BC)

I have come to believe that we can shape much of our lives through our thoughts and actions. I do not believe we are mere puppets or victims of circumstance. I feel that at the very least, we can control the contents of our own minds which in turn control the *essence* of our experiences. It's not easy, but we can—and must—endeavor to take note of our reactions to whatever is swirling around us.

Now, more than ever, we need to manage our stress. Life continues to get more and more complicated and the planet is evolving at lightning speed. It is my hope that this book helped you to learn some valuable ways to manage your stress, or served as a reminder of what you already knew but weren't putting into practice. I know that I need the constant reminders.

I believe that even with all of its travails, life is something to be savored and enjoyed, not something to "get through." We need to enjoy all of the wonderful things life has to offer, but keep things in balance and exercise moderation. (I, for one, cannot imagine a life without cake.) We need to ask ourselves if the indulgences are worth the consequences and be satisfied and content with whatever we choose. Or make new choices.

Let's take stock of our fears from time to time and see if there are any that we're ready to let go of. I'm thinking of giving spiders a second look. (Well, maybe.)

If we always maintain a healthy curiosity and continue to keep learning, we'll never grow old.

Let's take care of our bodies, otherwise, where will we live?

Bless your friends and loved ones for they are the foundation of your soul. They also know all of the dirt on you. Plus, you never know when you might need a kidney.

Endeavor to always keep an attitude of gratitude. Be *more* full of yourself ("I *know!*"), and brag a little. Your true friends will be happy for you and help you celebrate your victories. The rest don't matter.

Most importantly, try to find the humor where you can. It is one of our greatest gifts.

Remember that for the most part, living a life of joy is a choice. As my mom always said,

Most people are about as happy as
they make up their minds to be.

—Abraham Lincoln (1809–1865)

And always wear clean underwear.
I mean really.

By the way, did I show you this?

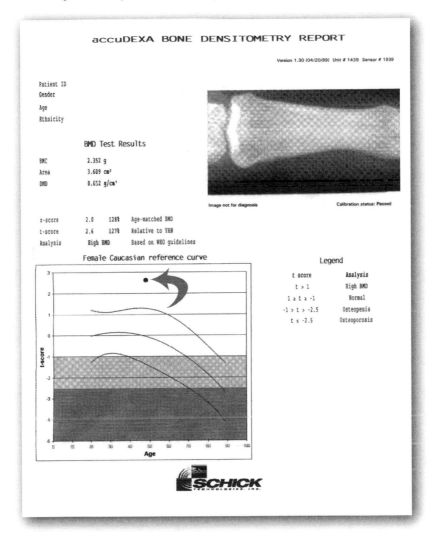

ABOUT THE AUTHOR

Kay Frances has shared her message to "lighten up, stress less, and take care of ourselves" in thirty-eight states and Canada for over twenty-five years. She holds a master's degree in business administration, a degree in physical education, and a fourth degree black belt in karate.

As a humorous stress management specialist, Kay teaches that healthy people who manage their stress and lean toward the lighter side are happier and more productive than those who choose not to.

When it comes to humor, Kay is the "real deal," having performed as a professional stand-up comedian for many years and appearing on a number of national television and radio programs. She also lived in New York City where she performed at the nation's top comedy clubs including the Improvisation and Catch a Rising Star.

When it comes to stress, Kay learned the hard way by engaging in every unhealthy habit known to man before making her way back to good health and sanity. She now feels compelled to help others on their journeys.

Kay travels the country giving humorous keynote presentations and stress management workshops. Her extensive list of clients includes 3M, Travis Air Force Base, Rohm and Haas Chemicals, American Red Cross, Discover Business Services, American Society of Military Comptrollers, Missouri State Teachers Association, Dickinson Health Care System, and many, many more.

When not on the road, Kay resides in her beloved hometown of Wilmington, Ohio. She enjoys a relatively low-stress life with her cat, Seisan—at least as low-stress as life with a bed hog can be.

www.KayFrances.com